African Son

Wambalye Weikama

This book has been published in print, e-format and sold on Amazon.com by KHAMEL Publishing.

Visit us on the web at:
www.khamelpublishing.com

ISBN: 978-9970-9453-0-6

African Son

Wambalye Weikama

KHAMEL
PUBLISHING

Foreword

Dear Sim,

Papa is sick again.

He needs your prayers. Things are not too good around here, and they only seem to be getting worse. There's very little money for anything... the house was sold and we have moved to the farm.

My father was not a complicated man. At least not the way I knew him. Many people compare me with him, relatives mostly, so I assume he was quiet and reserved. He never involved himself with Ugandan politics or the military although he had many friends in those trades. He was an insurance man who built a successful business out of the ashes of a bitter civil war.

He loved me and my sister Anna immensely and saw to our every comfort. I'm sure he loved our mother, too, because he never remarried after her disappearance when we were very young. It's only now that I'm older and he has passed that I realize I never really knew this man.

Sitting here watching his grave, I'm transported back to earlier days growing up with him, a single father of two. Of course, back then I had no concept of that social phenomenon.

He was never a confidante, counselor or buddy to us. Just a father, a guardian, really. He catered to our wellbeing and rebuked us where necessary and never raised his hand to Anna or me. He was gentle and aloof. The last time I saw him alive was the day I left for college in the U.S. He drove me to the airport accompanied by Anna and Aunt

Drusilla.

At the gate, we parted with words of encouragement and a handshake. That was it. I remember he was disappointed that I had chosen to attend college in the United States over the United Kingdom where he had gone

through the trouble of getting me a school. My desire to study international business came at a very early age. I loved the idea of traveling the globe, making business deals.

It was a passion that would inevitably separate Anna and me. Although we were twins, Anna having been born only five minutes after me, I regarded her as my kid sister. We went to the same schools and were in the same classes up until high-school. However, Anna's career dreams were in law, specifically corporate law.

The university in Kampala offered Anna's course but not international business, so we had to part ways. Our father had tried hard to interest me in medicine so I could stick around, but his efforts were in vain. Biology and chemistry were not my strong points and anything having to do with engineering was out of the question. I wanted to travel and close deals and nothing was going to stop me.

After completing high school, my father arranged for me to go to college in England. But I wouldn't hear of it.

"People don't go to England to study business," I had argued. "England is OK for medicine, or language, or something like that, but the U.S. is the place for studying business."

In my senior year, I got in touch with my friend Benya who had left for Washington State a year earlier. He was enrolled in the University of Washington there and would help me through the application process.

On my part, I completed all the relevant tests and

mailed the admissions office every required detail including flattering recommendations from my teachers.

The entire process was completed in a few months leaving only one major hurdle: the money.

I waited patiently for the perfect moment to approach my father who had already assured me that he did not have the time to go through the process of getting me another college.

One starlit evening while seated at the veranda and sipping some scotch, he invited me to join him and talk about my college prospects. This was no isolated occurrence.

However, when I glimpsed a rare touch of paternal exuberance in his tone, I seized the moment and brought out the file that I had compiled over the months. This, among other things, included my admission letter.

All that was remaining in the process was sending the money to the school so they could mail me the visa papers. He was shocked and surprised. Although unsure whether I was just being rebellious or really committed to pursuing my goal by all means, he gave me the benefit of a doubt. I had after all demonstrated a great deal of initiative.

In mid December of 1993, I left for the University of Washington. Anna went to Makerere University in Kampala, both of us pursuing our goals and for the first time in our lives separated by thousands of miles. My initial goal at the University of Washington was to prepare myself thoroughly for transferring into an Ivy League college for the junior year.

To achieve this, I had to tailor my program to be both competitive and rigorous. The issue of grades was no problem as I remained one of the top five students in all my classes with little effort and my professors knew me well and were quite friendly. For academic prowess, I earned the President's Award at the end of the school year and also received a community service certificate for volunteering weekends to tutor high school kids. I worked all the angles.

Surely there was no way Stanford would reject me. Getting there would not only prepare me for a dream career. It would earn me my father's respect and thereby legitimize my erstwhile rebellion.

Chapter 1

Anna's letter was a light blue aerogram type. Very brief, saying dad was sick and had sold the house. I remember sitting on the bus and going over it in my mind, confused, puzzled, perhaps a little angry. A lousy ride, gray skies, and noisy teens. I was on my way to the bank and the only interesting aspect of my day was the bank woman who I had grown fascinated with over the weeks. I was sure she would be there today.

As the bus snaked through the narrow streets, my thoughts oscillated between the bank and the ominous letter. As if possessed by dueling spirits, I defaulted to a vacant gaze staring into the near distance and not really seeing. Father was sick again and had sold the house in the city.

I was puzzled as to why he would sell the house he had built and lived in for fifteen years. Anna and I were raised there having moved when we were seven. We truly knew no other home. The previous house which we called the Blue Gate house was nothing more than a vague memory. We moved from there a few months after our mother's disappearance when all hope was lost. The house he had sold held countless memories that were the fabric of our childhood. It was our true childhood home and the place in which we came of age. Getting rid of it was like tearing away a large part of our lives, and yet he had sold it without mentioning it to me. I, his only son, hearing it from my sister. I knew it was not a money issue since my tuition checks were always on time. Something was awry and I could not put my finger on it.

Riding the bus guarantees one thing, scattered thoughts. The bus stops, someone gets on and you look up as they pass you. Noisy passengers notwithstanding. Disjointed thoughts strung together by bus stops. When the bus returned on Everett Way, it made a left on West Mall Drive towards the mall. I reminded myself to disembark at the bank. Often I missed the stop and found myself at the mall then had to walk back a quarter mile to the bank. That day Benya and I had a party to attend at the Greek village near the University. I was looking forward to it and needed to withdraw some money and deposit a tuition check. I hoped for a fun weekend.

My father had raised the two of us almost single-handedly. After the disappearance of our mother in the late seventies, Auntie Drusilla, our father's older sister, moved in with us to help keep house and babysit. Unmarried but estimable, she earned Groucho as a secret nickname due to her rebuking nature. She was a tough and strict disciplinarian. She was also a typical product of colonial Protestantism. Her type had been churned out like automobiles in their thousands by the Church Missionary Society in the fifties and sixties. Prodigies of Her Majesty's provincial tentacles, they were steadfast in their faith and religiously opinionated. Such was the nature of Auntie Drusilla. If any house rules were broken, she quickly pulled out a Bible and pointed out which of the Commandments had been defaulted then grabbed the culprit by the waist and pulled down his or her pants and pinched the thighs with such exacting viciousness that they were left smarting for days.

This kind of punishment accommodated all transgressions ranging from bedwetting to fighting. And woe unto you should you break the Ninth Commandment, for you received nine on your left and nine on your right. How she interpreted her penal code only Moses knows. Auntie Drusilla was indeed something else, but she had her good side, too. Somehow, one couldn't figure out where the nurturing stopped and the cruelty began. But she was kind. More like matriarchal. She was the mother we never really knew and, to her, we were the children she never had. As we grew older, she moved back to the farmhouse in Gayaza to look after granny and manage the farm.

Now dad had sold the house and moved to the farmhouse too. Why? I liked visiting the farmhouse. We spent almost every Christmas there with what appeared to be the entire clan. Uncles, aunts, cousins and other relatives always gathered there on occasions like weddings and holidays, and it was fun to be there on such occasions. Now it was going to be permanent and so would the presence of some relatives who stayed year round. I didn't like the idea very much. I thought my father should have consulted me.

Once inside the bank, I filled out a deposit slip and joined the queue. I was the last person in line and only one teller was in. As soon as I saw her, my heart started racing. She did this to me every time I came to the bank. This time was even worse because I was planning on asking her out to the party with me that night. Now that might sound simple, but I had only chitchatted with her previously, something like very familiar small talk. I was not even completely sure it wasn't extraordinary customer service on her part, but I was determined to push that boundary today and take it to the next level.

My pulse was relentless. I started setting up the conditions for my leap of faith. First, I made sure I was the absolute last person in line. Lucky for me it was a Saturday and the bank closed just after I walked in. This, too, was planned. Having someone behind me in line would seriously thwart my courage. I didn't want anyone overhearing me make the move and possibly get rejected.

The line continued moving and my heart raced faster. Only three people were left. Very briefly, she looked at the line as if to gauge how much of the queue was left. She

caught my gaze and I managed not to look away. I cautioned myself to act cool. After all, what was the worst that could happen? Right? Somehow I could not kid myself. Paranoia followed soon. What could I possibly hope to accomplish beyond making a fool of myself? What idiotic abstractions were my wily hormones pumping into my dormant brain?

I watched her closely and knew I really wanted her. I needed to get it across to her somehow, to breech the gap between our worlds. Her hair, so unpretentious, was loosely tied into a French braid. She wore no makeup. I surveyed her without concealment as she keyed away at the computer, examining her rich dark hair, big round earrings, hairline, nape, smooth skin. As I got around to the nose I noticed she was looking at me.

"Oh." It was my turn at the counter.

I wobbled forward and told her what I wanted then watched as she tapped the keyboard with grace. She said something about twenties and fives. I nodded and studied her soft sensuous lips. I wanted this woman and this was the time to lay out my practiced line.

"I'll be right back." She stepped out of her cubicle to pick something from the inner office. Her smile remained plastered on my mind.

On Saturdays, the bank employees dressed casually so she was sporting fitted dark jeans that accentuated her hips and some kind of baseball top with the bank logo on the left breast. I watched her return from the back room and decided I would ask her now.

"You know you can make the deposit at a machine to avoid being charged," she said as soon as she returned to the counter.

"I know."

She looked at me with what I hoped to be understanding then gave me a deposit receipt and the money I had asked for.

"Have a good weekend," she said.

"You, too." I turned and walked out of the bank a nervous wreck, angry and disappointed by my cowardice. It was raining and the parking area was almost empty. I decided to wait under the bank's roof instead of standing at the uncovered stop across the street. I looked at her business card which I carried in my wallet.

Romina, it said, a Customer Service Representative. Here I was, infatuated with a beautiful bank woman who was at least five years my senior and probably in love with some undeserving fool. What was I thinking? Was I just another disconcerted guy stunned by the familiar American beauty? I knew she was not married. Although she wore several rings, none was the fateful one. I figured she must have sensed that something was wrong. I always talked a little. Flirted a little. This time I was numb as a statue. On an earlier visit to the bank when we chatted, she had asked where I was from and where I went to school. She even asked if I liked the girls. "Of course," I had replied. That helped break the ice. She knew I had been in the country less than a year and had no girlfriend. My intension was to capitalize on that. Now I had blown it.

After waiting a few minutes and seeing no bus, I stepped into the rain briefly to peek around the building and see if there was any coming up the street. When I saw none, I returned under the shed. Just then, she stepped out of the bank and opened her umbrella.

"I'm waiting for the bus," I said, feeling trapped by her presence. I fumbled around for something to say.

"Ah . . . it's raining and there's no shade at the bus stop."

"Are you OK?" She regarded me with a casual smile.

"Yeah."

"Would you like a ride?"

"Ahm . . . OK. Thanks. I uh . . . ," I hesitated. I lived on Everett Mall Way, but if I said I was going south, and she happened to be going north to the freeway, there would be no ride. "Are you going up?" I asked.

"I'm going to Highway 99."

"Me too," I lied.

"You can drop me somewhere there." That was actually the general direction of my apartment, but I only lived ten blocks from the bank. Going up to Highway 99 meant returning by bus from wherever she dropped me.

"Good, there's my car."

We walked to a burgundy Camry and my nerves resumed their circus. After driving a few blocks in silence, I thought to engage her in some fruitful conversation; otherwise the ride would be in vain.

"How long . . ." I started.

"Do you . . ." she stopped in mid sentence. We were talking at the same time. I giggled nervously.

"Go ahead, please." I shifted in my seat trying to relax. "You were saying?"

"I was wondering if you have family here."

"No. I have no relatives in the States."

"So you live by yourself?" She came to a complete stop at a red light at the second intersection.

"I have a roommate. He's from Uganda too."

"Does he also go to the UW?"

"Yes."

Again silence as we watched the traffic in front of us. The rain had subsided to a steady drizzle. I kept stealing short glances at her as she concentrated on the road. She was obviously a product of a mixed marriage, probably Black and Hispanic. The Hispanic features were evident in the dark curly locks and goddess-like hips, and though she was not glamorous, she was positively sensuous. In fact, just sitting next to her in the car was like a sexual experience for me. There was a mysterious quality about her that seduced me completely. It must have been that intrinsic certainty radiated by many older women whom I found powerfully attractive. I was irresistibly drawn to the mystery woven in their poise and experience and could only unravel it by being close to the woman, seeing the look on her face in high passion, hearing the sounds she made in ecstasy, and penetrating her innermost thoughts. That way the mystery would be laid bare from the inside out.

"Have you lived in Seattle a long time?" I broke the silence.

"No, I moved here only two years ago from Pennsylvania. That's where my family lives."

"Hmmm . . . interesting. I'm going to Pennsylvania this summer."

"Really? Where?"

"Philadelphia. I have a friend at U Penn who invited me over for a few weeks."

"You will like it."

"I hear it's very humid during the summer."

"Yeah, it can be awful sometimes but it's good . . . different."

We approached the intersection to Highway 99.

"Do you like your job at the bank?" I tried to shift the subject.

"Someone has to do it."

"I couldn't possibly handle dealing with that many people in a single day."

"You get used to it."

"When are your days off?" I asked flatly.

"Why?" She looked at me questioningly.

"I like to come when you're there."

"Is that why you come on Saturdays?"

"I'm sure to see you on Saturdays."

"Do you have to see me?"

"I feel good when I see you." Her gaze remained fixed on the road.

"So . . . Where?"

"What?" I was puzzled.

"Where do I drop you?"

"Oh, sorry." I looked around for a convenient spot. "At that McDonald's, if you can find a spot."

"I thought you were going home."

"I am. I want to get some fries first."

She pulled off the road. Before leaving the car, I mentioned the party at the university and asked if she would come with me.

"Why do you want me to come with you?"

That caught me off guard.

"Well . . . two reasons." I fumbled on. "I think it will be fun. You will like it."

"A frat party? I don't think so. "

"But . . ." I searched for convincing words but none

were forthcoming. Then she made as if to drive away, but I held firmly onto the door.

"What's the second reason?"

"What?"

"You said two reasons."

"Oh, the second reason is I like you and would like to do something together."

"How about just dinner sometime?"

"Even better."

"Call me at work next week," she said at last with a broad smile.

"All right." I hesitated briefly then reluctantly shut the door.

"Thanks for the ride," I said softly.

She backed up then, before she turned the car, our eyes locked briefly with unspoken messages. She smiled again and rolled towards the road. No sooner had she joined the main road, than I saw my bus pulling up to the stop across the road. Because I did not want her to see me going to the bus, I pretended to walk into McDonald's while watching her car at the intersection. As soon as she turned and disappeared, I ran after the bus and crossed the northbound lanes praying no policeman would see me. When I reached the middle of the road, the bus started pulling out. I cut across all lanes almost getting hit by a speeding minivan. Once safely across, I continued racing towards the bus and shouting at the driver. Too late. I was thoroughly soaked and out of breath. Being in no mood to sit around waiting for the next bus, I started walking briskly back home with a broad smile of satisfaction.

At the beginning of that summer, I visited a friend in Philadelphia, and Romina who had a brother there, gave me a parcel to take to him. She said his name was Gary Shawn and gave me his address in Pine Street. I went there the day after I arrived. Although it was evening, the temperatures were awfully high and the air stagnant. The building was a three story yellow brick with a basement floor. Some of the buttons at the front door had no names, so I pressed the one marked 2C, which was written on the package.

"Yeah?" A female voice.

"I have a message for Mr. Shawn," I said.

"There ain't nobody here by that name."

I stepped out on the street to confirm the address then returned and pushed the buzzer again.

"Who's there?" Same voice.

"I have a parcel for 2C."

"I'll be down in a moment."

I waited five minute before someone opened the door. She wore only jean shorts and a bra. No shoes. After looking me over briefly, she asked if I was the parcel guy. I said I was. Then she held out her hand.

"Sorry, I have to hand it to Mr. Shawn himself."

"Where is it from?" She asked suspiciously.

"Seattle."

"Wait a sec." She disappeared into the dark stairwell and the door closed slowly. A few minutes later, the door opened again. This time it was a man of medium height and light complexion, wearing dark-rimmed glasses. I could not see his features very clearly because the hall was dark, and he was partially concealed by the door.

"Are you Simon Peter?" He asked in a deep voice.

"Yes." I was shocked at hearing my full first name from a stranger. Everyone called me Sim.

"You must be Mr. Shawn," I semi-inquired.

"Romina said you have something for me. I was expecting you yesterday."

"Yes . . . Here . . . parcel and letter." I handed over the items.

"Thank you very much." He studied the address on the letter and retreated into the darkness. Slowly the door closed. I stepped back onto the sidewalk and headed up the street.

Two weeks later we met again.

Philadelphia was still very hot, but I was intent on touring the historic city on foot. It was by habit that whenever I felt thirsty, I would wander into the nearest public building and look for the drinking fountains. I had done so at the Convention Center near China Town and the Ritten House Theater two days earlier. It was pure coincidence that when I felt thirsty on Vine Street, one of the buildings close by was the Free Library of Philadelphia. So I went in. I just as easily could have gone into the adjacent Family Court or the Science Museum around the corner. I walked into the library and looked around for the fountains, which I located on the second floor. Not eager to re-enter the heat, I idled around the library and uninterestedly happened into the humanities section located on the main floor. When I got to the section on religion and philosophy, I saw him. He was wearing the same dark-rimmed glasses and a brown bow tie. His coat was neatly draped over the back of his seat. The desk was littered with thick volumes of which two were open; one had Arabic script and the other was a Bible. As if sensing my presence, he looked up and acknowledged me by name. I did likewise and joined him at the table.

"My sister won't accept the new truth, so she still calls me Gary."

"And what is the new truth?"

"Malik Mohamed X." He paused, observing my reaction. "You can call me Malik."

"Nice to make your acquaintance, Malik." We shook hands. He was affable and we talked for almost twenty minutes. Mostly he asked questions and made observations. He inquired about my country and my mission in America. He also asked about my family and religion. Just before I left, he asked if I knew about The Honorable Minister Louis Farrakhan. I said I did and only then did he offer some information about himself. He told me he was one of the Minister's assistants and in a few weeks would be seconded to Seattle as the Minister's emissary.

"Come tomorrow and watch the Minister talk. He has an important message for people like you and me." At first, I was reluctant to accept the invitation but changed my mind, not wanting to antagonize our delicate acquaintanceship. He gave me the address to the Civic Center and bade me good day.

Chapter 2

The entire first year at the university was nothing like I had anticipated while in Uganda. I had been so abundantly lectured about America and had forcefully psyched myself into believing I was prepared for college in America that I failed to see the truth in the lecture spiels on the eve of my leaving. Many people talked about the difficulty of life in America, of hardship and a need for strength, but to me, these were merely parting suggestions. Perhaps they applied to others who, unlike me, were asylum seekers with families to fend for. I was just a foreign student on an adventure and with an unwavering gleam in my eye for the Ivy League. I took the advice in good faith but dismissed it as passé counsel from relatives and the like.

It was not until the middle of my first quarter that I began to get a sense of disconnect that rapidly degenerated into desolation. I felt as if I had been transplanted into some mechanical system with a numbingly metronomic routine that saw me up at five o'clock every morning and back to bed at twelve o'clock nightly. I always woke up early, showered, ate a peanut butter and jelly sandwich with coffee and rushed to make the first of three busses by 5:45 a.m. The rest of the day passed with similar drudgery that included four hours at the university's burger stand and three evening busses back to Everett. Life seemed to pass by in between those moments. I felt a longing for the life I had had in Uganda. School was tougher there, but it was fun. Here I was some kind of zombie with no real friends except Benya, though, unfortunately, I rarely saw him since he worked mornings and went to evening classes. I dreamt about going home for a visit but knew I could not because it was prohibitively expensive. My father had decided that I would visit home at the end of my second year before transferring to Stanford. I looked forward to that day every day.

In the first six months of school, my relationships with other students never went beyond casual niceties even though I wanted real friendships that could outlive a common curricular. To some extent, I had anticipated this situation as I was no longer surrounded by close friends I had known for many years. They were scattered all over the globe now. Farouk was in Sydney studying architecture. JT's dad had shipped him off to Bombay to study Computer Science. Jonnie and William were in London; and the others were at the university in Kampala. Only Benya and I were in Seattle and, even then, we rarely saw each other. We lived in the same one bedroom apartment and attended the same school but only saw each other twice a week.

This was the first American shock for me. The other thing that nothing could ever have prepared me for was the feeling that I had become the guy in the classroom that everyone regarded as the provincial kid. The poor African kid who had to work to make ends meet and was in this school only by way of philanthropy. I was deluged with the most patronizing gibberish by my American classmates:

"Oh you have such a lovely accent", "Oh you are so sweet"

"I would like to visit Africa someday." What flagitious

bullshit.

Tell that to your moronic poodle or your neighbor's retarded kid, not Simon Peter Wasswa. I did not need charity; my credentials were solid and far beyond the flabbergasting nonsense these ignoramuses called sophistication. I was well traveled and understood the world on a level they could never dream of achieving and yet they made me feel as if I was a nobody.

In Uganda, I was not only in the best schools but was, at the same time, one of the most prominent students socially and academically. Here the role reversal made me bristle and fomented a rush of resentment towards any friendliness accorded me which I perceived to be merely charitable. Almost always my accent was commented on as if it was the only identifying aspect of my whole personality. Even answering a teacher's question became nightmarish. I had to strain to pronounce words only to see the teacher straining to understand what I was saying. Conversation was agonizing and I avoided it as much as possible. By the end of the second quarter, I was emotionally exhausted and only beginning to understand that fake pleasantries were the norm in this culture. Here intimate language and expressions of affection were no more valuable than dirt and were disgustingly farted out all over the place and scattered on the wind.

The pleasure in meeting interesting people was lost on me. I always misread their signals only to find out that they did not even remember my name a day following a seemingly productive interaction. Other things I thought would bring me pleasure, such as shopping, only exacerbated my desolation. Back in Uganda, it was a badge of exclusion to have certain clothes or American brands which garnered admiration because they meant you had means. Now wearing them was meaningless because there was no one to share the pleasure with. The unique clothes and fashion trends that had been treasured and rare in Uganda were stacked ceiling high in numerous department stores. There was absolutely no pleasure in wearing them here since their symbolism was nil and no one really cared for them as we had in Uganda. With that pleasure gone, I settled into a routine of school and work. I saw Benya even less because he had hooked up with a Kenyan girl called Halima that I could absolutely not stand.

Not only was Halima bedraggled and unhygienic, she was excruciatingly dim-witted. Perhaps her only redeeming qualities were her good looks and physical attributes, which she flaunted generously. Naturally, given that bonus, I could not fault Benya in sticking with her. It was no secret between Benya and me that I did not like his girlfriend, but this did not complicate our friendship, and she and I managed to remain civil to each other even under the difficult boarding arrangement.

When I first arrived from Uganda, Benya had allowed me to room with him in his one bedroom apartment in southern Everett. Although he never charged me rent, we agreed that I would buy groceries and be responsible for my share of the bills. This was very generous of him and it worked well both ways. I bought a sleeper sofa and slept in the living room and had my computer desk there, too, where I spent hours nightly doing homework. Things were quite okay until Halima came into the picture. First, it was obvious the place was too small for two lovers and an extra, that being me. Very quickly Benya bought a second TV and moved it to his room for more intimate TV watching with her. For that I applauded him. But before long Halima took over the place. She filled the fridge with junk food and colonized the bathroom. Her knickers were all over the place and, occasionally, she left blood on the toilet seat. This was the dealbreaker for me, but being a quasi-guest in Benya's apartment allowed me little say on issues pertaining to his girlfriend. I stayed with Benya through the middle of my sophomore year before moving to my own apartment near the University, thanks to the job Romina had secured for me.

Romina and I had been dating for about nine months when I started working at the Nation of Islam office in Seattle. Apparently, a few weeks after moving from Philadelphia, Malik had sought me out against Romina's protestation. Since telling her about our chance encounter at the library and the Nation of Islam rally I attended, she was suspicious of his intentions. I never understood her trepidations because I was fairly impressed by him and thought him very intense and articulate. His name, however, did not come up again for several weeks until one evening when she said she had secured me a new job with him.

At the time, my job at the University was hopeless and paid peanuts. Every weekday after class, I worked at the Student Center burger stand for four hours, making burgers and scraping grease. Often, when Romina met me after work, I was thoroughly exhausted and smelled of pickles and grease. So she decided to strike a deal with her brother. She would only put us in touch if he promised to give me a decent part-time position at his office. He promised to do so and, a few days later, we met for a job orientation.

The office Malik set up was located in Madrona, the heart of Seattle's black neighborhood. The objective of this office was to boost awareness of Nation of Islam doctrine in Seattle and to spread the gospel according to the teachings of The Honorable Elijah Mohammed, founder of the Nation of Islam, the main theme being the rebirthing of spirituality in black America. It was paramount, therefore, that the office be strategically located since they would be holding many awareness and recruiting seminars.

Malik himself never spoke at seminars. He organized them and coordinated such details as security and accommodations for the guest speakers and their entourages, who were mostly higher ranking ministers commissioned by the head office in Chicago.

Also high on his agenda was increasing the readership of their propaganda magazine. When the magazine's distribution increased in the Seattle area, Malik's office leased a hangar at the South Boeing airfield along Interstate Five where FedEx planes delivered the bi-weekly magazine on Sunday and Wednesday evenings. Here, the magazines were re-sorted and packaged for street vending. They were then delivered by van to the office in Madrona where youthful, well-dressed vendors picked them up the following morning before hitting the streets.

I worked at the office in the afternoons three days a week as a program assistant. My job consisted of data entry and clerical chores that included answering phones, invoicing, typing up itineraries, and a host of other office issues. It was not unusual to sit at the computer for four hours at a stretch. I did this for a couple of months before my responsibilities were expanded to include picking up the magazines from the hangar.

By then, my financial situation had improved, and I had moved out of Benya's apartment in Everett to the Maple Leaf neighborhood along Lake City Way. That way my commute to school was reduced to ten minutes, and I was only a few minutes from Romina's place.

One evening during the autumn midterms, I found a note at the office asking me to meet Malik at the hangar.

As was customary, my Wednesday responsibilities consisted only of delivering the magazines from the hangar to the office before it closed. It was not unusual to be late in picking up the van to make the delivery as was the case that day. So I wondered why Malik wanted to meet me at all. Rather than speculate, I got the van keys from the receptionist and took off. Malik would know after all, that I was doing my midterms and often stayed late at the library.

It was approaching 7:30 and the night was dry and chilly by the time I turned onto Airport Way. I continued south along Airport Way and passed the flight training schools and airplane rentals. At the Pacific Avionics building, I turned right and passed a security gate into the airfield grounds.

The private hangars were lined to my left where I drove around to the back.

In the space where I usually parked the van was a light Cessna aircraft. Next to it was Malik's Chevy Yukon. No one was outside the hangar, but the door was slightly open and the lights were on in the inner office where I heard voices.

The hangar's office was a big cardboard cubicle about ninety square feet with a table in the middle that was littered with old magazines and newspapers. There were no windows in the whole building.

The man standing across the table from Malik regarded me without expression and returned to his activities. He appeared to be weighing something packed in small plastic bags on a medium sized digital scale that stood on the table. He picked the packets out of a bigger plastic bag on the floor and, one by one, weighed them and neatly packed them in brown corrugated boxes marked "Stationary Supplies." Malik was seated in one of the chairs around the table.

"Did you get my message?" Malik asked then, without pausing for an answer, went on. "Please close the door and have a seat." I tried to make myself at ease and sat in one of the chairs next to the table.

"I delayed at the library. Sorry," I said. "Traffic sucks, too."

"Don't worry about the magazines, they've already been delivered." I shot a quick glance at the corner where the pile of magazines usually stood. Malik turned in his chair and faced me squarely. "I have a business proposition, Simon." He paused for effect. I had long given up on encouraging him to call me Sim like everyone else did.

Seeing no reaction from me, he leaned forward slightly and went on. "It's very simple and straightforward but requires utmost confidentiality and accountability." He paused again, his eyes unblinking. I remained motionless but attentive. "Whether or not you agree to the deal, no one gets to know about it, understood?"

"Understood."

"Not even Romina." I nodded. "Not now, not ever," he pressed on, his eyes burrowing into mine. I nodded again. I knew Malik was aware of the relationship between Romina and me. Still, he never breached the issue to either one of us. This was the closest he had ever gotten to saying,

"I know you and my sister are doing it."

I remained attentive, indicating that I was interested in hearing his proposal.

"This is my business associate, Torres. He lives in California." The man who hitherto had neither said a word nor been introduced had already filled seven "Stationary Boxes" with the small brown packets. "Torres owns the plane you saw outside; he will be flying in merchandise once or twice a week. What we need is someone to receive that merchandise when it gets here and take it to a distribution center on Lake Union."

"Kind of what I've been doing with the magazines," I remarked but the humor was lost on him.

"Yes, kind of like the magazine stuff, only you don't have to do the magazine stuff anymore. You won't even have to work at the office anymore and for every trip you make, you'll be paid two hundred dollars." He paused again for effect, and when no reaction was forthcoming, he continued.

"That's a lot more money than you're making now and you'll have more time for your books." Again, he paused slightly and then asked, "What do you think?"

He leaned back in his chair and regarded me keenly as if trying to read my mind.

$200 a trip twice a week would be only slightly more than the $300 a week I was making at the office. As far as I could tell, the nature of this enterprise was on the dodgy side. First, it was obvious Torres was not packing pencils and erasers. Second, the hush, hush nature of it meant it was a high liability enterprise. Now, unless Malik thought I could not count well, there's no way he would have thrown out a number like that expecting me to jump at it. I was sure a little more money for the service he was asking of me was worth his while.

"Four hundred dollars per trip and I'll ask no questions."

"What?" Malik sat up in his chair and Torres stopped whatever he was doing and eyed me with a trace of amazement.

"I assume there are a number of questions about this enterprise that you'd sooner not have me ask, is that right?"

"Correct," replied Malik.

"So I think, instead of two hundred per trip, you pay

me four hundred and I'll ask none of those questions. I'll pick up the merchandise whenever it comes in and deliver it promptly and confidentially."

Malik shifted his eyes from me to Torres who looked equally impressed by my shrewdness.

"What do you think about that?" he asked Torres.

"That's cool," Torres replied in his first spoken words since I had joined them.

"That's cool," Malik repeated to me. "So you're in?"

"I'm in."

"All right, then. Here's how we'll do it. All pick-ups will be here at 8 p.m. or later. The magazine people are long gone by then. You will use the van since it's always available in the evenings."

"I will also need to know the delivery schedule," I said.

"No schedules," Torres interjected.

"No specific delivery days?"

"No." Again Torres. "Get a beeper, I'll page you whenever the merchandise is ready for pickup." Torres's English was good, but heavily accented. He was definitely a rich son of a bitch. After all, he owned a plane, wore a solid gold watch and a flawless leather jacket. I assumed he was Mexican.

Presently, Torres completed packing the boxes, and we started loading them into the back of the van. Altogether there were nine and a half boxes. I estimated each box to weigh about twenty pounds. Whatever it was that Torres had flown in from California that evening would therefore total well over a hundred and sixty pounds. Somewhere in the recesses of my mind, questions kept popping up. *What on earth was I doing? What was I thinking? Was I thinking at all?* The questions were infinite, but I knew above all that a deal had been struck and I had given my word. I would rationalize my decision later. Right now, my duty was to follow Malik and Torres in the Chevy so they'd show me where to make this and subsequent deliveries . . . and, oh yes, fetch $400 for a few minutes' worth of work.

The Cessna was wheeled into the hangar and the door closed. I got into the van behind the Chevy and followed them towards the freeway. The time by now was 8:45 and the night still dry and cold. After driving about twenty five minutes, we exited the freeway. The so called distribution center was a houseboat on Lake Union, accessible through a combination lock gate and a wooden gangway that extended fifty yards into the lake between several houses.

Malik and I stayed in the cars while Torres went to the house. A few minutes later, he returned with a short, gold-toothed Hispanic man he introduced as Mario. Mario immediately started unloading the van, and I helped him move the merchandise to the house. Except for Mario's sparse bedroom and the two office desks in the living room, the house was empty. After all of the boxes had been moved into one of the bedrooms, Malik gave me $400 and said henceforth all shipments brought in would have to be verified by Mario before I got paid. Mario would be the one to hand me my money. It was settled. I departed $400 richer and without the smell of grease in my hair. The rationale for my decision was complete. I would open an account in a different bank so Romina would not find out about my weekly deposits.

On the way from parking the van, my thoughts returned to the nature of this enterprise. Getting paid $400 for making a mere twenty five minute delivery represented a substantial risk factor attached to whatever was being transported.

What was it in this case? And how far in the dark was I? How could I assess a situation which I knew nothing about?

I had to find a way of establishing what the merchandise was. For an extra two hundred dollars, my associates, as I thought of them now, had bought themselves a "no questions asked" policy. But, of course, the questions bounced around in my head. For instance, *what the hell was the merchandise in the boxes? Surely it was not stationary. Could it be drugs or some other contraband? Was I being naive to even propose options to those answers? How deep was Malik into this? And how long had it been going on? What about Torres?* He appeared to be close to Malik, but I had never seen him at the office. *What was his stake in the enterprise? What reason would I give Romina for carrying a beeper?* I had no major responsibilities. I would have to think up something.

It was after nine that night when I drove to Romina's place, aware that she wasn't expecting me; however, I did not feel like spending the night alone. She was in a robe and getting ready for bed when I arrived. Nevertheless, she took a piece of veggie quiche from the fridge and heated it in the oven for me.

"If I had known you were coming, I would have prepared something decent."

"I'm not hungry."

"You're always hungry," she said and left the kitchen, joining me at the sofa. "So why the surprise?" she inquired.

"Pleasant I hope." I dodged the question and gently massaged her feet.

"Of course." We looked at each other in the dim TV light, her look inquisitive, mine devious.

"I have to be up at seven, you know."

"And so you shall," I replied flashing a naughty smile. Whereas she was sometimes overwhelmed by my youthful energy, I knew she appreciated its compensations. She had recently transferred to a branch nearer than Everett but was responsible for opening it and had to get up very early.

After eating my oven dinner, I asked about Malik, much to her surprise.

"What about him?" she asked candidly.

"Anything. Like how he was as a kid or what he did before becoming religious."

"He is not religious. It's a façade. Don't let him fool you." I was slightly taken aback.

"I think you're mistaken. You haven't been around him lately. He's really the fundamental religious type."

"I don't need to be around him," she went on "He's my brother. I grew up with him." She paused slightly "Why all of a sudden are you interested in my brother's background?"

"I have my reasons."

"I don't feel like discussing Gary now," she said. My curiosity had gotten the better of me, and I was not about to give up the subject so I cajoled her for a little information. She went into the kitchen and poured herself a drink then returned to the sofa where I continued rubbing her ankles softly.

"Gary was in prison when he converted to Islam."

"Prison?"

"Yes, state prison. He did two and a half years in New York for drug stuff."

"That's serious shit."

"Very serious," she concurred. "He was always in and out of trouble. Always. If there's something you've discovered, you should tell me."

"No, there's nothing at all," I lied. "I'm just curious."

"Trust me. I love my brother, but from a distance. Right now he's your boss and that should be all."

I wondered what she would do if she learned about

that night's developments. I changed the subject and asked
her to turn over so that I could massage her back. When
the movie ended, I went into the shower.

Chapter 3

I continued delivering Malik's merchandise through
the holiday season. By now, Torres was flying in three
times weekly and bringing more stuff. Romina had asked
me about the beeper I carried, and I told her I needed it
because the magazine deliveries were sporadic and I had
to be reached whenever they arrived. The beeper was the
best way to contact me. She believed me and that was settled; however, personally, I was starting to get a little jit-
tery about the whole business. Things were starting to get
more sketchy for me in many ways. First, Malik insisted
that I change my delivery route every week and tell Mario
what route I had taken. Then there were these guys I started meeting at the boathouse. It was always the same two
husky white guys who looked as if they were waiting to
pounce on the merchandise as soon as I left. Mario never
cared to tell me their names but only referred to them as
Mr. Gemma's guys. The air surrounding the whole operation became so tense that I wanted out. I was willing to
forego the money just so I could sleep without fear that
the police were going to bust in on me for involvement. By
now, I had dismissed any naïve ideas about what kind of
racket I was caught up in. The hard part was how to quit.
I surely could not just walk up to Malik and say I was tired
of his $1,200 a week. That was no option. I had to find a

clever way of ending it.

Even my relationship with Romina was getting strained. One day, she found $800 in my jacket and asked what the money was for. I had to think quickly so I told her it was tuition money, but then I had to explain why I was walking around with $800 of my tuition money in cash. I told her my tuition check had arrived ahead of time, and I loaned some of the money to Benya who paid me back in cash earlier that day. I doubt she bought my explanation but, at least, she could not disprove it. I was getting weary of the lies, and it hurt knowing that the person I was lying to cared deeply about me and would not do anything to harm me if she found out the truth. I had told lies to protect previous ones and had even amassed standby lies that might come in handy.

I disgusted myself and resolved to tell no more lies. If she asked anything henceforth, I would be forthright and take her into my confidence. Naturally, she would be upset, but I would explain that I only intended to deliver the merchandise until the end of the quarter which was in four weeks. By that time, I would have saved nearly ten thousand dollars and would have devised a gracious way to exit Malik's enterprise.

I never had problems speaking with my sister before she moved to the farmhouse. I called home weekly and often we spoke for hours. Since moving from the city, however, she was impossible to reach. Occasionally, I could reach her on the single phone in her dorm, which was very unreliable. We agreed I would call her at Aisha's house in the city during school breaks. Aisha and Anna were best friends and had known each other since sixth grade when Anna and I transferred to a new school. Calling Anna at Aisha's was quite involved.

I'd call Aisha and find out when she expected to see Anna next so I could coordinate the phone call. If she wasn't expecting her, she went to the farmhouse and asked Anna to come on a particular date. Sort of like an appointment. And then I'd have to wake up at four in the morning to make the call. All that was OK. The only problem was that something was not working out now. I had been trying to get in touch with Anna for a month and could not. Every time I called Aisha's house, I was told she was at school, and when I called their dorm, no one who picked up the community dorm phone cared to help me find either one.

One day, a girl who answered the phone said Anna was not at college because she had requested a dead year. Now, requesting a dead year is no small deal at a university in Uganda. It meant a student could leave school for a whole academic year and start off the following year where he or she had left off the previous year. In Uganda there was no such thing as simply accumulating credits in order to graduate. You matriculated into a prescribed course with

dates and classes assigned ahead of time for the duration of your course. If you did not come to class for more than one term, you were officially dropped from the university and had to re-apply as a freshman to get back into that course no matter how close you had been to graduating. In order to be eligible for a dead year, students had to present a convincing case to the dean's council as to why they wanted to take a year off from school. Cases eligible for a dead year had to be due to some extreme circumstance.

By now, it was mid December and I was getting ready for my exams. I was extremely anxious to hear from home and eager to know what problems Anna was having. I tried to call my father at the office but was told he was out of the country. I started getting really bad headaches and spent more time with Romina. It helped to have someone close by. I never talked to her much about my family, but she was a comfort. She knew I was worried about my sister and tried to comfort me.

The last time I had spoken with Anna there had been no indication that anything was wrong. All she said was they needed my prayers. Because she was not a religious person,

I took this to mean that things were a little tough. I had never spoken much with my father on the phone even when they still lived in the city. I called every week to speak with Anna and, occasionally, he asked to talk to me. Mostly our conversations went like this:

"Did you get the money I sent?"
"Yes Dad. Thank you."
"Are you working hard?"
"Yes, I am."
"Your sister misses you," or "The family misses you."
"I know. I miss everyone, too."

That's as far as our conversations went. My father never said I love you or miss you. Never. The closest he ever got to that was "the family misses you." Our relationship was never so insecure as to warrant him re-enforcing it with "I love you's." I never even said it to my sister nor she to me. We were all in the same mental space as far as our relationships with each other. The only thing my father did when we talked at length was lecture me about my obligations to the family.

Like any African man with a son studying abroad, his horror was my returning home with a foreign wife and kids who did not speak a lick of the language. This truly kept him up nights, and I never had any doubts about his expectations of me.

The call came in the middle of the night two days after my finals. I had dismissed my alarm and was just beginning to adjust to staying up late and sleeping in front of the TV. I staggered to the phone and picked up the receiver.

"Hello."

"Hello?" came the reply after some seconds. "May I speak to Sim?" It was Aisha unable to recognize my sleepy voice.

"Hey Aisha, it's me."

"Sim?"

"Yes?" Irritated.

"Did I wake you?"

"No. Not really. I've been trying to get in touch with you forever. Is Anna OK?"

"She's here with me. She wants to talk to you."

"OK. I see you finally got my one thousand messages."

"I'm afraid, Sim, she has bad news."

"Bad news?"

"Yes," she answered uncomfortably.

I guess this was it. I had felt it coming for months. Something was wrong. What was it? Was she sick? Was granny dead? I was scared to talk to her.

"OK" was all I could say.

"Sim?" I could tell she was sobbing. My heart sunk.

"What's going on Anna?"

"Dad's dead, Sim," she paused. "He died last night."

How could this be? This is not what I had sensed. He was out of the country. She was away from school.

"What are you talking about? They told me he was out of the country?"

"No he wasn't, Sim. He has been in treatment for a long time. He had AIDS, Sim." She was now crying openly into the phone.

"WHAT? AIDS?" I could not understand what was going on. "Why are you telling me now? Why now Anna? People don't just drop dead from AIDS."

She cried louder and tried to explain in incoherent phrases.

"I tried Sim . . . I even hinted in the letter, but you did not understand." She blew her nose loudly and went on. "How do you think I felt? I wanted so much to tell you, but dad begged me not to."

"Why not?"

"I don't know why."

"Who is at home now?"

"Everyone."

"What about Ellen?"

"She arrived just before I left."

"She hasn't been staying at home?"

"It's complicated, Sim," she hesitated briefly. "You know how people here are . . . I mean, at home. They haven't made it easy for her."

"And granny, how's she taking it?"

"Badly, she's also very sick. Please stop asking all these questions."

"I'm sorry. I wish it were a bad dream."

"Sim . . . auntie said you don't have to come for the funeral. There's no money at all. Everything went into medication for dad and granny."

"I can find some money," I protested.

"You could put it to better use. What is done is done. Life has to go on."

"I'll see about that. Right now I'm confused. Ask Aisha

to be around at five o'clock your time. I'll call and tell her what I've decided."

"OK, but be strong Sim. Do you have anyone to be with?"

"I'll be fine, don't worry about me. It's you I'm worried about."

"I'm OK this end. You know I'm not alone."

So he was dead. One moment a life is there and the next it's not. What happens in between is fleeting. The worst thing one can say to a bereaved person is life goes on. But does it really? For me life ended with my father's death. Life is not just living protoplasm. It is hopes and dreams. The absence of a lighthouse and a guiding beacon is the beginning of death. I sat thinking for hours, then slipped into a horrible nightmare...

I was walking in a dark town with very long narrow streets. I hastened my steps and tried to look behind, but my neck was stiff. Everyone in the street was headed in the same direction as I was, but I could only see the figures in front of me without making out their faces. They were scattered along the narrow street, each alone and dressed in long, dark trench coats with stiff collars. Some wore hats, old bowler hats, and walked with a determined gait. No one looked behind. The street narrowed and the buildings surrounding it blocked the light, leaving only a glimmer at the end of the street where it opened out into some kind of public square. There were no cars in sight, only scattered trash and garbage cans littering the narrow street. Occasionally a wild cat or rabid dog crossed my path and disappeared among the garbage cans. Soon the street narrowed into an alley with a solitary dark figure about twenty meters in front of me. I tried to shout at him, but my words were muffled. I even tried to run, but my legs were heavy. By now, the alley was a thin corridor, so thin I could touch both walls. The corridor opened into a wide valley several feet below where the man preceding me had disappeared. I approached cautiously and looked at the valley, which sloped towards a dried riverbed. The floor was scattered with shrubs and red giant lotuses with thick purple stems, and was infested with diverse, ugly creatures that crawled between the plants and the shrubs. Some of the creatures were giant, slimy, centipede-like slugs. The smaller ones resembled wingless cockroaches. Other creatures were half-breeds with dove tails and toad heads. Nothing in the valley had legs. so they slithered, leaving slimy trails. The smell from the valley was suffocating. I tried to turn around and leave but could not. My neck was still stiff and I couldn't make a complete turn. Then, from the corner of my eye, I saw a figure emerge from the valley. It was dressed in a hat and a long, dark coat. I realized it was the same one that had preceded me in the alley. I looked on, entranced, as the figure approached me. About twenty five meters away, the figure stopped and watched me. I noticed it was my father. He held out his hands inviting me into the valley, but I hesitated and tried again to turn around. Then he bent down to pluck a giant lotus, and I saw another face on the back of his head. I was horrified. The face was that of a beautiful woman. Nice sad eyes and a wide, noble nose. The cheekbones were high and well oiled. Those features looked familiar, but I could not place them. The mouth however, was that of a squealing horse, with big, grey teeth. My father extended the plucked lotus toward me as one would a bouquet of flowers. Giant slugs and creatures scurried out of the severed stem while others burrowed deeper inside. I was terrified. I started moving backwards into the narrow alley, and my father followed me with outstretched hands. I hurried backwards because I couldn't turn around. The alley darkened and my father started running towards me, hands outstretched with big bugs and lizards falling out of the lotus. I tried to shout in the darkened alley, but I couldn't nor could I move faster. Soon my father reached me. He grabbed me by the collar and shoved the lotus plant inside my shirt . . .

I awoke from that dream sweating and confused. I jumped off the sofa and tremblingly switched on the light, then tried to remember how much of it had been a dream. The valley......the dark alley......the dark streets.......the phone call.....the phone call.....was that part of the dream?

"Ooh no."

The following day was grey and dull but not rainy. I was haunted by guilt and obscure emotions and hadn't slept a wink since waking from the nightmare. I had been angry with my father for a long time for selling the house, and all the time the poor man was sick and dying. I wanted to cry, to throw myself down and sob painfully, but I couldn't. I had slept after being told he was dead, and now I could not even cry. Could there be a more complete betrayal? My subconscious hounded me with accusations. I tried desperately to remember the last time I saw him. To relive that moment, but I could not. I had walked away with a handshake and told myself not to look back. It would be a sign of weakness.

And now he was dead. Why was it that the day I set out for college, the day I went to build my future, would be the last day I saw my father? I desperately wanted to see his face. Just once before the ground swallowed him. Even the body in a coffin would bring closure.

That afternoon, I called Malik from my apartment and told him what had happened. He was surprisingly support-ive and inquired if there was any way in which he could be helpful. I told him I was considering flying home for the funeral and might be gone for a few days. Although I never mentioned it, I had made up my mind not to work for him when I returned. After talking with Malik, I called Benya and left a message on his machine then went for a walk.

Although it was only eight days before Christmas and the holiday fever high, this activity never permeated my spirit. With a heavy melancholy settling in, I walked north towards Roosevelt Way and Romina's office. Somehow I felt calm, as if I had shed the initial anxiety that weighed me down and resigned myself to hope. I knew my life had changed forever from the moment I answered that phone, and yet, I had no idea where it was headed. I kept walking.

I arrived at the bank a few minutes before closing and remained outside waiting for Romina near her car. A question I had fought off all day returned to assail my mind. If my father had died of AIDS, then whom did he get it from? I knew better than to point fingers at such a time but the where or who question haunted me like bad air returning persistently to the lungs.

Along with this question came memories that had long been suppressed.

Within a five year period in the mid-eighties, Uganda endured several military coups in bitter conflicts between the dregs of Amin's demolished military and newer externally sponsored insurgents dueling for the heart and soul of Uganda. In my opinion, this period was perhaps the most traumatizing of Uganda's turbulent times. Although we had lived through an eight year period in which hundreds of thousands were systematically exterminated by Amin, a period that was brought to an end by a bitter civil war, I could never equate those earlier days with what was happening now.

Obviously, Anna and I were younger during the war and our perception of reality was skewed. Now we were older and not immune to the paralyzing fear that followed every coup, every stampede in the city, every burst of random gunfire and bloodcurdling shrieks in the middle of the night.

It was an age of fear and torment when all it took to have your life flash in front of you was a firm knock at the door in the middle of the night. This was the life we lived then. Dreading the night, not knowing what evils it would unleash upon the sleeping souls. Indeed, just praying and hoping to make it through one day.

During those turbulent days, business men of all calibers were routinely detained with accusations of sponsoring rebel activity or outright treason for plotting to overthrow the prevailing government. Such wanton accusations were obviously heavily politicized and not uncommon. The basic logic was that if you were successful and did not contribute towards a perceived cause, you were a threat to it. My father did not escape these insane accusations and was held for five weeks with several others in the basement of a military barracks outside the city. When he returned home, he was weak and skinny, but he encouraged us that he would be fine and, in a couple of months, he was healthy again.

He never talked to us about the horrors he endured in the five weeks that he was detained, but, over the years in conversations with my uncles, I learned what life in the barracks' dungeons was like for the detainees. Most of them were victims of witch hunts by the government that had overthrown Idi Amin, or they had held government positions in a toppled regime. Others, like my father, were

48

influential business men who were perceived as a threat.

During the night, detainees were dragged from the dungeons, one at a time, for interrogation and torture. Some of them never returned. Others were tossed back into the dungeon bleeding profusely, and their counterparts were ordered to scrub the blood stained floor every morning. If any of the detainees died, as did many, their bodies were hauled away in the middle of the night in the back of army jeeps. On several occasions, some detainees, including my father, were taken to the barracks' clinic, supposedly for medical checkups. Here they were injected with substances that were said to be good for their deteriorating health. These checkups were not optional and neither were the injections.

Many people believe, in fact, that the injections they received were deliberately tainted with deadly substances including HIV. It was feared that the government had devised a method of killing people without having to take them out into the woods and shoot them. In the five weeks that my father was detained, he received three of those injections.

Although the rumor about the HIV tainted injections had never before appeared credible, I believed it that day because I was desperate to know who was responsible for my father's death. I was sure the same people who had taken my mother had now deprived me of a father, and I was consumed with fervid hatred. The same bastards who had promised democracy and civil justice were, in fact, raging murderers. They had fooled the people and gained their support in removing a mad dictator only to replace him with tyranny. I wished I could confront them and make them suffer the way I was. I would wipe out their loved ones, too, and make them watch as I mercilessly slaughtered their mothers, wives, and children. Perhaps only then would my sorrow diminish.

I was sure my father's death would rouse the same sentiments in many of my relatives. However, some would think differently. Despite constant pressure from several family members, my father refused to remarry after my mother's disappearance. For Anna and me this was nothing to complain about. In our rebellious minds, the thought of a stepmother was totally unacceptable. Even Aunt Drusilla's moving in was met with resistance, but before we could find a way to make her life a living hell, she had pinched our little thighs up and down until they were totally scarred. Soon everything fell back in line for us and the fading memories of infanthood eroded many memories of our mother.

I envied Anna for her memory. Unlike me, she remembered a lot more about our childhood than I did. Some of her memories went back to the time when we were only three years old. Perhaps the earliest memories I had of my mother were of the times she organized lavish birthday parties for Anna and me. The parties lasted all day with us kids playing until we collapsed from fatigue. I also remembered outrunning her one day in the front yard of the Blue Gate house. I challenged her to a race from the gate to the doghouse in the corner of the compound and won. Naturally, I was jubilant. I couldn't have been more than four years old. She did many things to make me feel like a winner and they always worked. The exception was when it came to competing with Anna. She never let me challenge Anna to anything where I might win.

After the war and our mother's disappearance, our father immersed himself in business and built a successful insurance company that assured our comfort. He sent us to nice schools and lavished us with niceties. But if his prodigality tended towards spoiling us, our aunt pinched us back into shape.

As we grew into adolescence, I realized that my father was only human. He was a man with needs in terms of companionship. How he satisfied his needs, I never ventured to speculate. I completely locked from my mind issues regarding that aspect of his life. Several years later, Anna and I reconciled ourselves to the fact that the woman we always saw in his company was, in fact, only one step away from being our stepmother. Still we persisted in calling her by her first name, Ellen. Nothing could have conceivably altered that. Although we never cultivated a close relationship with Ellen, we liked her. We loved it that she had no direct control over us and never threw her weight around when it came to matters relating directly to us.

But when it came to a conflict with our father, she often arbitrated. One day it was the issue of college that caused sparks. My father was adamant in his insistence that I attend college in the United Kingdom.

"America is expensive," he had protested. "Do you think I pluck money off trees?"

His great idea was for Anna and me to go to the same college and perhaps even do the same degree. In a stupid rage, I had told him off and said something about Anna and me dying together of old age. We did not talk for weeks after that until Anna told me that Ellen had talked to him about letting me pursue my dreams, even if it meant going abroad. I felt so ashamed that I apologized to him in the manner that Aunt Drusilla had taught us by accompanying a spoken apology with a written statement expressing regret for my misconduct.

If Ellen was not staying at home while my father was sick and dying it was only because she had been barred from doing so. My family, dominated by Auntie Drusilla and granny, was very conservative. Not only were they infectiously Christian, they were also very old fashioned. For them, a relationship not sanctified by marriage was proximately scandalous. For that reason, I imagine Ellen could not be allowed to spend the nights at the family house.

Not even during my father's final days. Anything like that would have adulterated the family name, or so they thought. I even suspected some relatives were pointing fingers at her saying she had brought the virus into the family. Every family has people whose occupation is to accuse and gossip. Their slender fingers identify you and their long mouths sentence you. What does one do in the face of such hostility? My thoughts were startled by Romina's voice.

"Are you OK? What are you doing here?"

"Waiting for you."

"You don't look well."

"My father is dead."

"Oh my god, I'm really sorry. When did you find out?"

"My sister called last night."

"What are you going to do?"

"I'm going home."

That afternoon we found a travel agent near the university, and I bought a return ticket on a flight leaving the following evening. I would arrive home two days later in the early morning after flying for eighteen hours.

Motherless since childhood and now fatherless, I was lost and uncertain. There was absolutely no one to turn to for guidance and to find my path I would have to feel around blindly hoping not to stumble.

When I returned to my apartment, I called Aisha with details of my flight and asked that Anna be at the airport when I arrived. Afterwards, I sat at the bedroom window and watched gray buildings through leafless twigs. In the distance, I heard sirens and watched a dull winter dusk fade into a freezing night.

Chapter 4

The nine hour flight from Seattle to London was typical. All I remember of it was doing nothing but remaining in my seat unable to eat, sleep, or partake in the host of puny services offered. I was a zombie lost in thought and just waiting to get to my connecting flight home. During that time, I thought a lot about my family. I had many relatives, very close ones like Aunt Drusilla, granny, and a host of uncles and cousins. I could not legitimately argue that mine was a small family or that there was no support structure. However, in my heart, my real family was the immediate one with only Anna left. It was really scary to think of it that way. Just me and my sister. That was all that my world consisted of now. I knew she was in as much pain as I was.

For sure I had felt her pain long before I knew what was happening. It had always been that way. Somewhere we were one, connected by a mystic force that could only be explained by having come from one cell and simultaneously shared a womb. Any filial disconnect I might have felt with the absence of our parents was immediately restored in her since she was the only representation I had of them. She was my entire world now, and I needed her more than ever. The tragedies and crises over the years had made us stronger as a family with each being a pillar of strength in the lives of the others.

The first crisis I remember was the liberation war from Amin's regime. By then we were still a complete family unit and spent three months holed up in the house as the war raged on. We survived that one as a family. Then came the misery that followed our mother's disappearance. The long days of hoping turned into months of despair and, to make things worse, our favorite uncle and younger brother to our father died in a freak rally car accident not too long afterwards. It was a time of turmoil for our family but all through it our father was there taking care of us. Now all we had were memories and each other.

From the plain of Kitemu, a narrow, rugged road winds off the highway and disappears into the hamlets of Budo. Two kilometers later it emerges as a thin thread twisting upwards around the imposing hill of Nagalabi, running over rock aggregations and enduring two perilous hairpins. At the peak of its upward toil, it branches out, the left fork falls to the valley and rolls into the villages of Kisozi and other small ones, but the right fork leads you to the summit of Nagalabi from which resides the ancient King's College.

Upon this summit, in bygone days when the air was clear, the king surveyed the expanse of his blessed dominion. From the northerly spur, if he looked westward, he saw as far as the shrubby hills of Buloba and the seven hills on which the city currently stands. From the southerly spur, he beheld virgin forests on rolling hills and humble villages extending southward beyond Masaka until the sky swallowed them.

With a sweeping leftward glance, a most magnificent valley prostrated before him and offered its expanse and splendor. The slopes rolled eastward from under his feet into a thriving plain that stretched forever. In the unseen distance the plain would rise again to shoulder Entebbe and embrace the rugged shores of the revered Nalubale. In submissive reverence, the king would rub two drops of saliva on his breast and offer a sacrament to the spirit of Nalubale so that in her tempestuous tantrums she may spare his loyal subjects as they hunted in the bowels of her waters.

In olden days, King's College was a popular destination for children of kings and nobility from the Great Lakes kingdoms. Here, in its Victorian structures and vast campus, they came to make alliances amongst their kind and to drink of the white man's knowledge. The College, however, failed to defend its tradition when, in 1978, it was occupied by Sudanese rogues imported as mercenaries to aid Idi Amin and his blood-thirsty cohorts as they were being driven out of Uganda. Its physical elevation had presented it as a strategic military base against the liberating forces that advanced from the south.

Anna and I were only six years old when we drove up the winding road with our mother to pick up her younger sister, a teacher at the college. The Sudanese had given everyone on the hill exactly forty eight hours to vacate or get shot. That applied to both students and teachers. Our mother's sister packed only a couple of bags and, in no time, we were off the hill and back in the city where we lived.

Several years later Anna and I would return here for high school, but, unfortunately, we would not make that trip with our mother. In fact, the trip to pick up her sister was the very last ride we had with our mother. When we got home, our father wanted to shift the entire family to the farmhouse for the duration of the war, but in a matter of days, the situation was so bad that driving around or out of the city was dangerous. Soon, even walking in the streets was impossible. Amin's government had become so desperate that they started conscripting civilians at random and sending them to the war front to join his losing forces. A 4 p.m. curfew was imposed on the whole country and, like many families, our own was stranded in the city. The dark cloud of war was upon Uganda.

My recollections of the months that followed the trip to King's College are still vivid. On three occasions, our mother left home for periods of up to four days and always came back at night wearing the same clothes. One night upon her return, we heard our parents quarreling in the bedroom. It was obviously a heated argument, even though they tried to keep their voices low. We never found out why the two had quarreled, but when our mother left in a week and returned after two days, she never went out again.

For almost three months, we remained locked away from the outside world and never opened the windows or curtains during the day nor turned on the lights at night for fear of attracting hostile attention. Occasionally, our father ventured outside to get some of the basic necessities we subsisted on. How or where he got them, I had no idea, but going outdoors during those days was of paramount risk and called for a lot of courage. On such days, our mother held her breath until he came back. If he delayed in returning, she would go into a panic, and her very being would transform into suppressed hysteria. She would then lock herself in the bedroom so as not to affect us.

Anna and I were not bothered much by what went on in the outside world. All we knew was that it was unpleasant for the unpleasantness was manifested in the house. The anxiety radiated by our parents made us apprehensive, but the outside noise and destruction affected us little even when the house shook so violently as to almost collapse.

Occasionally, men dressed in army fatigues came to the house and talked to our parents in the corridor. Mostly, they asked questions and then hastily searched the house quietly but thoroughly. They would then leave as stealthily as they had come. Sometimes they left with documents acquired from our mother. They had small attaché cases in which they stuffed the documents or photos that she gave them. One day, the same men who had come during the day returned late in the night and questioned her about some slides they had brought with them. They projected the pictures on the wall in the darkened living room and made her sign papers.

Whenever strangers came to the house, we children and our mother's sister were confined to the bedroom. Any information we got was by way of eavesdropping or pretending to go to the bathroom at timed intervals. First, I would go and in a glance or two spy what was happening in the living room. Then it would be Anna's turn. We exchanged information on what we had seen and then pressed our ears against the bedroom door to listen. If our mom's sister tried to stop us from doing anything, we would throw a tantrum.

What those men usually came for, I had no idea, but no stranger ever returned after the night of the slide pictures. At night, our parents spoke in near whispers among themselves and our mother's sister. At specific hours, they crouched close to a radio with the volume adjusted to a minimum. During the radio ritual, no one made a single noise. The dancing flame from the tiny candle sitting on the radio illuminated a trio of near trance-like masks that were their faces, and the giant shadows against the walls made facial distortions in rhythm with the lazily dancing flame. The aura was somber and hypnotic.

The radio ritual was a mystery to me. All I heard was

an inaudible monotone that struggled through an incessant maze of irritating radio static. Often I considered tuning the radio correctly when no one was listening but feared inviting the war to myself should I fumble with the radio and lose the station.

During those days, Anna and I slept in one bed in our parent's room. Our mother never wanted to let us out of her sight. Occasionally, in the thick of night, the noise from artillery and gun fire would suddenly die and, for a while, not a sound could be heard. Time appeared to stand still and the darkness thickened as the silence intensified to where you could almost hear it. It was like a manifestation of the war goddess suffocating us with darkness and numbing our senses with stillness. We all listened because no one really slept. It was at such moments that the war became real for Anna and me as darkness was our sworn enemy.

The country remained in shock for a long time after Idi Amin and his junta had been deposed, but, slowly, people started putting together the remains of their lives. Soon our parents arranged for our schooling and tried to jump-start our father's business. One day, a few months after we had resumed school, our mother left and never returned. Whatever happened on that fateful day, only God knows. She just went missing. Announcements were made on radio and search teams were deployed, but every effort to find her was futile. Our father employed all means and facilities available to him in trying to secure some information regarding her whereabouts but all was in vain.

Ever since the system of forceful change of government was adopted in Uganda, one thing remained a favorite of every new administration. Witch hunting. People who held any political position in any administration were in mid-step to exile. If they chose to stay after governments had changed, they became victims of witch hunts and were systematically fazed out of society. Either they mysteriously disappeared or bogus charges were brought against them by the government, and they ended up in prison. It was not too surprising that these same people had a high propensity for death from "short illnesses" while they were incarcerated. How this was achieved one wonders, but whichever way you looked at it, they were off the scene in a matter of a few years.

After the war, many people disappeared as a result of persecution. Some went into exile and many simply vanished never to be seen again. Along with those was our mother.Many theories emerged since then speculating on her disappearance, but I heard the most disturbing one during my first year in high school almost ten years after her disappearance.

A friend and I were seated at the tennis courts waiting for a game. Our families were close and the parents had known each other a long time. Whatever subject we were discussing while waiting for the game is lost to me because of what he said.

"My folks say your mother used to work for Amin's intelligence. Is that so?"

Those words penetrated my heart and exploded it, wringing from me emotions I never could have imagined to possess. I stood up quietly and went to my dormitory leaving him unsure what offense he had committed.

Amin's intelligence agency, the State Research Bureau (SRB) was only comparable to Papa Doc's Tonton Macoutes in Haiti or the former East Germany's Stasi. Not only did they have an effective, well-funded network, they were also notorious death squads and assassins who saw to the disappearance of more than 500,000 Ugandans in the eight years that Amin ruled.

Although I knew my mother held a government post in Amin's regime, I was firm in the belief that she had absolutely nothing to do with Amin's intelligence network and, even as her image faded with time, I was sure she had loved us very much. Any suggestion from anyone that she had worked for Amin's SRB was enough to make me hate that person forever.

Due to a delay in London, I arrived in Uganda at nine o'clock the following morning. The sun was up and the air was warming as I alighted from the plane and walked to the terminal, carrying only a stuffed backpack and a pair of sunglasses. The custom's lady who took my line yawned repeatedly and asked me few questions before letting me through.

The lounge was full of people waiting for relatives, but I spotted Anna immediately standing in the back with one of my uncles. I wish I could say my embrace with Anna was intense but it was quite anti-climactic. I had anticipated it all along, imagining what kind of state she would be in. Instead, she was a little detached albeit jovial. No dramatic breakdowns or displays of overt emotion as I had feared. We talked a little and followed our uncle to the car, both of us taking the back seat. I felt there was some disconnect between us and sensed anxiety on her part, as if she was waiting for something from me. I studied her face, thinking she looked more mature and bigger than she should. Then, without saying a word, she pointed to her belly with both her index fingers and looked at me questioningly.

"Well?" she said following my puzzled look.

That's when it hit me that she was pregnant. Anna, my little sister, was pregnant and all I could come up with was,

"Too much breakfast?"

"What?" It was obvious she wanted me to say something, to make some kind of comment, but I could not come up with anything.

My brain was completely locked. The next couple of minutes were probably the most uncomfortable time I ever experienced with my sister. I was completely dumbfounded and so was she, but luckily, our uncle came to the rescue and started briefing me about the funeral arrangements. Apparently a short service, conducted by the parish priest, was to precede the funeral. Many people were expected to attend the four o'clock burial since our father had many friends in the business community. One of the people expected to speak was the Minister for Trade.

My father had been a well-known man in both the business and political circles of Uganda. During the days when the current administration waged a guerrilla war against Amin's successors, his participation in that struggle had been instrumental but not direct. He had been terribly discontented with the dictatorship and, at a risk to himself and his family's wellbeing, had contributed funds towards the struggle and also set up a secret fund to help the families of exiles. Many people sympathetic to the cause contributed to this fund and his effort had been lauded by those whose children and dependents benefited from it. It was only natural that a political heavyweight like the Minister for Trade should attend the burial to express the government sentiment. When my curiosity about Anna's situation piqued, I started in a roundabout manner.

"Are you still dating Chris?"

"If you mean was I impregnated by Chris. The answer is yes," she replied very curtly. "But this is my child. My child alone." She looked out the window at the speeding hills. I looked at my sister and all I could think is I don't know this woman any more. *What had happened to her in the three months since we last spoke at length?*

"Anna, Look here." She turned and looked at me. "Do you recognize me?" She nodded slightly "Then talk to me please. I don't recognize you anymore."

She looked out of the window again and started sobbing quietly. Seeing that she was deeply pained, I moved over and embraced her, then she broke out crying violently on my shoulder. In between sobs she said things and mentioned names. All I could gather was that Chris her erstwhile boyfriend had insisted that she get an abortion and also that Aunt Drusilla was constantly denouncing her for her "sinfulness."

Seeing my sister in this condition made me regret the day I left her. I could only imagine the sheer hell she had been through in my absence. While our father was sick and painfully wasting away and she was bound by her word to him not to mention a word of it to me, she was pregnant by a cowardly bastard whose only objective was to get her to some butcher so he would not have to be a father. In addition to all of this, she had to endure Aunt Drusilla's zealotry and self-righteous tirades about her sin and how she was going to hell for it. She was absolutely alone and had dealt with it by leaving school and growing a protective shell that excluded even me from getting close to her.

I hated my family for doing this to her—for not being there to support her when she needed them the most. Instead, they had chastised and judged her.

So what if my father was sick and dying? So what if there was already a tragedy befalling the family? Could they not see that she was pregnant with hope? That she was the family's salvation? An expect-

ant mother in a time of grief? What did that Bible teach my aunt? To revere death and disdain life? I hated my family.

A few months before my father's death, in one of our extensive phone conversations, Anna had asked me about children. She already knew about Romina. This was no secret between us. So she asked what I'd do if Romina were to get pregnant. I answered frankly that I loved Romina and, therefore, would let her have my child. I even mentioned that I did not really care what our father's opinion would be. That was my honest feeling, despite the fact that I knew Anna's position on abortion. She was vehemently anti-abortion, not because she was persuaded by some political creed. Rather, she was absolutely terrified of it.

Anna's horror of abortions began five years earlier when we were in boarding school. At the time, junior girls had mentors from senior classes for whom they performed basic chores like cleaning rooms and washing clothes in exchange for such favors as protection from bullies or help with class work. This was the same with us boys. Anna's mentor was a slender girl named Becca. One day, near Christmas break, a vicious rumor started circulating among the senior girls that Becca was pregnant. Anna heard it from one of her junior counterparts, and she believed the senior girls were just being malicious because Becca was the most beautiful girl in the whole senior class. However, something strange happened.

It was a Sunday and all the girls had gone to attend service, which was compulsory for all students. We always dressed neatly in Sunday uniforms and left the dormitories before nine o'clock. No one was permitted back into the dorms until after twelve o'clock when the service ended. That day, Anna left chapel early with an excuse that she had a terrible stomach upset and needed to rest. When she got back to the girls' dorms, she went to the senior girls' latrines, which she preferred because they were always well scrubbed.

On entering the latrine building, she heard a whimpering sound in one of the latrines. So she moved in the direction of the sound. At the door of the latrine, she listened intently at the sound coming from inside and realized that whoever was inside was saying, "I'm dying," between muffled gasps for air. Horrified, Anna bashed in the door and what she encountered was a scary sight. Lying on the floor in a pool of blood was Becca wearing only a white T-shirt, turned red and folded at the chest, exposing a bloody torso.

Her skirt had been jammed under the latrine door to prevent blood from flowing out.

Her legs were spread above the latrine and her bloody left hand was holding a long wire jammed inside her vagina from which blood oozed freely.

Not knowing what to do, Anna tried to jerk the wire out of her friend, but Becca cried out in excruciating pain and more blood came out in thick coagulations. With that, Anna knew her friend would surely die. She ran out of the latrine building to the school nurse's house, which was close to the girls' dormitories. The nurse who appeared to identify the problem immediately, told Anna to collect bed sheets from Becca's room and bring them to the latrine where Becca was then bundled in them and carried to the nurse's house. Anna was then instructed to scrub the latrine and drop all the extra linens inside before the girls returned from chapel.

Later, the following evening, she learned that Becca had been hospitalized for severe blood loss. The new rumor was that Becca had eloped with an older man but Anna knew better. Now, here she was being asked to do the same thing by her neglectful boyfriend.

I held onto Anna for a long time until her tears faded.

In that time, I knew we were one again—that her pain was
mine, her sorrow, mine. I knew she understood every
word I could not say to her.

"Thank you," she said.

The ride from the airport continued in silence. I had
many questions for her, but I thought asking them would
tantamount to harassment so I looked ahead thoughtfully,
watching the landscape speed by. Nothing appeared to
have changed in the time I had been away. The one hour
ride from the airport seemed like an eternity, and the closer
we got to home, the faster my heart beat. I imagined how
the people I found there would look at me, trying to see
what state I was in or what my reaction would be when I
saw my father's body. Would they be disappointed if I did
not break down in tears? Sure, I wished I could release my
anguish, but the tears remained locked inside, depriving me
of appetite and sleep. My eyes were bloodshot, not from
crying too much, but for not sleeping at all in two days.
Anna looked as if she had almost exhausted her tears, but
even with her puffed eyes, she radiated more strength than
I could muster. All I wished for was to see my father before
the earth ate him up.

I looked forward to reuniting with his image if only
by looking at the strong features that characterized his
face. Only then would I accept the bitter truth that he had
passed.

As we approached the gravel road leading to the farm,
I asked Anna what our father was like before he died.

"Was he in too much pain?"

"I think so, but every time I looked at him, I felt as if
he had transcended pain. It only showed when he was being fed."

"What were his last words?" I asked.

"I was giving him water and he said he was tired, then he slept and never woke up." We fell silent again. I reflected on my father's last words trying to interpret them and wrest from them a spiritual message that might provide me with comfort and assurance, but they only deepened my sense of resignation.

Our mother's memorial consisted of a statuette and an epitaph that read "devoted wife and loving mother we, shall forever miss you." It had been erected in the small family cemetery a year after her disappearance when all hope of finding her was lost. The day the statuette was erected was the only time I ever saw my father cry. Anna and I were only seven at the time and we, too, cried fiercely, not because all hope of finding our mother was lost, but because our father was crying. He cried openly in front of people and spoke words that I do not remember.

Now, standing in front of the memorial, I surveyed the small cemetery which was getting crowded. In the far corner, was the grave of my little cousin who had died of measles as a baby. There was also the grave of our uncle who had died in the motor racing accident many years ago. He could not have been more than twenty years old and was unmarried and owned no property. In front, near the tiny gate, were graves of great uncles and their wives, people who had lived so many years ago and some of whom I had only seen in very old pictures in the family album. The space next to my grandfather's grave was vacant and was obviously granny's. She, too, was very sick and old. The pattern in the cemetery was predictable, and I could easily tell where my own grave would be.

Next to our mother's monument, I watched as shirt-less men toiled under the noon sun to put final touches on our father's grave. At four o'clock, his remains would be laid to rest and with them would be the part of me that represented optimism. The four men worked diligently and without emotion, their sweaty torsos prominent with tough muscles that spoke of ceaseless laboring. Like many others around the village, these men moved in teams doing odd jobs for their sustenance. They cleared fields, assisted at construction sites, and dug graves. Most of the money they received from working was spent on booze. Even as they worked, I doubted their sobriety, although they appeared efficient.

This team of four had been selected by Isingoma, the farmhand, who having worked here for eight years knew the village well. These were his friends. They never accepted money for digging graves. Such money they said brought bad luck. Instead, they expected to be given food and liquor for at least one week. So they worked tirelessly in anticipation of the evening meal and boozing session.

The only time you ever saw them sober was when they played soccer during the inter-village league or when they went to the Forest of the Snake on hunting trips.

From the small cemetery, I walked up to the house. It was almost two o'clock and many people had arrived for the funeral. Cars were parked all over the compound and along the gravel road that ran alongside the paddocks. Many of our friends were present, too, some of them having spent the night helping around the house. At the entrance to the living room, I removed my shoes. Many people were seated on the carpet around the coffin, which was on a platform in the middle of the room. They were mostly women dressed in traditional tunics and singing funeral hymns.

For the third time, I looked inside the coffin to see if I could capture the image that eluded me the first two times. I looked through the glass casement at the body, but even this time, the man I saw inside was not my father. All that was recognizable on his face was the small scar across the brow that had always been there. The skin had paled and the eyes were hollowed pits. I was overcome with despair knowing I was going to bury my father without seeing him as I always knew him. Not even in death.

No matter how often I returned to look, there was a part of me that could not connect with what I saw inside the coffin.

Life had provided my father with sufficient reason to be courageous and, beyond that, to yoke his courage on struggle and faith. Yet, in its vileness, his life had turned and reduced him to a rueful figure. A body wasted by a microscopic bug, the strength of his soul eroded. Indeed his last words were true. He was tired. Tired and unable to sustain a struggle that began at his mother's breast only to end in prime age with his mother watching. Betrayed by life.

Just before the funeral service started, Aunt Drusilla gathered the immediate members of the family for a final prayer in what had been my father's nursing room. It was important to Aunt Drusilla and granny that we hold this prayer in the room where our father's spirit had left his body. Altogether, there was me, Anna, Aunt Drusilla, granny, one of my father's brothers, and his young twin daughters.

Aunt Drusilla led us in a long prayer for the dear departed and for the family at large. She prayed that God forgive Anna her sin and also for granny's health because she was very sick. She asked God for strength to see the family through the long difficult days ahead. She even prayed for herself and for courage.

I felt sorry for Aunt Drusilla. Being in charge of the household during these trying days had totally drained her.

She had lost weight and her age showed, and while she was obviously sorrowful, her unwavering faith kept her staid so that she never showed much emotion. She handled all funeral arrangements and busied herself by delving into every household detail, from delegating kitchen duties to coordinating parking. I knew this was her way of postponing the inevitable breakdown—the moment when overpowering grief and anguish wash over your whole being. I had been there several times already.

After Aunt Drusilla's long prayer, it was granny's turn. At the age of eighty three, granny was completely blind in one eye and suffered from rheumatoid arthritis and diabetes, and her blood pressure had to be measured at least twice daily. She had spent most of the previous days in her dying son's room, sitting on a straw mat next to his bed. She read a few short verses from a vernacular translation of the earlier King James Bible, an aged volume frayed at the spine with a red, threadbare page marker.

The Bible had been a wedding present from a missionary priest more than sixty five years earlier in this very house, but in an age lost to oblivion and reduced to fragmented memories. She read in the dim light refusing to be reminded that her sight was failing. She read verses from Isaiah and from the Apostles. From Exodus she recounted the plight of children of Israel and God's promise, "I will take sickness away from thy midst . . . the number of thy days I will fulfill." She read of the suffering of Job and lamented with David. With Jeremiah, she asked the Lord why her pain was perpetual and her wound incurable. Every day she had watched her son fade until he ceased being her flesh and blood, but the sole object of her spiritual plight. Why had her cries gone unanswered?

Only through profound pain that agonizes the mind and crushes the soul, do we mortals begin to glimpse who

we are as individuals and examine the nature of our existence. The pain becomes a beam of light that pushes us to
the edges of our psyche and then shines inward allowing
us a glimpse of who we really are, what we are capable of,
and where our faith lies.

My grandmother's grief was not isolated to this one
tragedy. She had produced six children and had outlived
four of them as well as her husband. Granny came from
a long line of dreamers. Not dreamers in the traditional
sense of idol-mindedness but more like seers. It was a he-
reditary trait that was passed down through the generations
with every generation having one of these seers who com-
muned with ancestors and even perceived future events
through visions as they slept. In granny's infancy, she had
been the seer. From the age of nine until sixteen, she was
the medium through which the mortals of her family com-
muned with the spirits of the ancestors. At solemn family
gatherings and occasions when communing with the dead
was crucial, she was there to perform. This was more like
an office than a talent. It was designated by ancestry and it
was never clear who this person would be. It fell randomly
on boys or girls but was pretty well established by the time
one got into adolescence.

When she was sixteen, granny met my grandfather
who, at the time, was traveling with a group of British mis-
sionaries as a guide and interpreter. Two months after they
met, granny was persuaded by the Christian way and was
baptized. She eventually married my grandfather, a man
twenty five years her senior, and together they left the
village and moved here to the farm to start a new home.
From that time onward, her life was devoted to serving
God and her husband. Any suggestions of communing
with the dead were perceived as satanic, and she insisted
that she had been saved by God's grace and delivered from

the gripping forces that evil spirits had on her as a child.

Granny's family never forgave her for abdicating her ancestral obligations and abandoning them. Because such a travesty could not go unpunished, many believed the tragic deaths of her children were a result of ancestral retribution. I imagine this was the most trying factor of granny's faith, that even as she buried child after child, she remained steadfast in her faith and only during the most painful moments did she dare to question the promises of her God.

At the end of granny's prayer, we recited the Apostles Creed and Psalm 23 . . ."even though I walk through the valley of the shadow of death, I fear no evil for thou art with me. Thy rod and thy staff, they comfort me." Then holding her one on each side, Anna and I guided granny to the tent were the funeral service was about to begin. Most mourners were gathered in a shelter erected inside the compound while many others sat outside the shelter enduring a light drizzle that interspersed with the afternoon sunshine.

The famously fat Minister for Trade, Honorable Francis Kaani, stood up after a family spokesman had given a brief eulogy. The Minister's face was grave and his appearance simple. He wore a dark coat with green elbow pads, and his shirt was unbuttoned at the neck revealing overlapping layers of fat. His young wife sat beside him dressed in a dark tunic and colored butterfly glasses. The Minister adjusted his trousers and pointed to the coffin and said in a soft voice.

"Today Uganda buries a great son." He paused and surveyed the crowd. The attention he commanded was undivided. He read the official government message and narrated how the deceased had been a pillar in the revolutionary struggle that led to the second liberation of the country. He reminded all how several families had benefited from the courage and valor of this man who at the height of the struggle had taken it upon himself to protect and guarantee the wellbeing of the families of exiles. He said he was particularly sorrowful because his own family had been sheltered by the deceased when government goons burned down his house several years back.

The Minister spoke long and modestly, and people remained attentive and sorrowful, but before he concluded his speech, he detoured into political rhetoric.

During periods of emotional trauma, the mind alienates reason and draws a delicate line between passions. In split seconds, men slay their wives, rage becomes lust, and admiration transforms into hatred.

Such was my state of mind when the Minister, instead of continuing his eulogy, switched completely to something akin to a political campaign. I started hearing words like "GDP," "we ushered in a new age," "your mandate" . . . words employed by piggish politicians to delude the masses. Had I been aware of the forthcoming council election, I might have been lenient in my condemnation of the Minister, but that was not to be.

I wanted to stand up and leave, which was impossible, so I sat and eyed the Minister with distaste. My father had been completely abandoned and where, a few minutes earlier, I had seen a nice man mourning the loss of a friend, I now saw a foolish ingrate and hated him.

Why did it have to be this swine anyway? Couldn't the government have sent someone else? I questioned how a lousy guy such as the Minister had even won the previous council election. His record was revolting and his scandals legendary. He was always in the news and tabloids scandalizing the administration and getting away with it.

This honorable slab of fat should have shown some

respect for my father. While he scurried into exile like a rat, my father had sheltered his wife and protected his children from his enemies. Now here he was at my father's funeral promising to lower taxes. I wished he would burn in hell.

When the moment came to return ash to ash and dust to dust, Anna and I threw in the first handful of soil followed by granny and Aunt Drusilla. Granny was once again overcome with grief. She knelt next to the grave and broke into a heart rending lament.

"Why? Why? Why, my son? My very own flesh, why? Why must I live, only to bury my own? My God, what did I do? Why should I labor twice to remove my own flesh from the womb and to return it to the earth? Why? Where do I turn?" She cried out her heart and mourned deeply, saying "Why?" again and again, but it was a "why" to which there was no "because," for it was not a question but a deep rooted lament, the lament of a bereaved mother, of a hen losing her chick to an eagle, of a lioness losing her cub to a stampeding herd, of a woman losing her child to an epidemic.

And so she cried for all the world's sufferings, for all those who suffer injustice and loss, for all those who have grieved like her and for all those who are yet to grieve. Everyone cried with her. Slowly two uncles moved her to a couch in the living room, where she was given a pill to control her blood pressure.

Many people broke into a mournful anguish, but I stayed put, anger having drowned out my sorrow. Quickly I walked up to the house and shut myself in Anna's room still brooding over the Minister's offensive speech.

A few moments later Anna confronted me.

"What's wrong with you?" she asked, closing the door behind her

"What?"

"How could you take off before the funeral is over?

People are shocked by your behavior."

"Who cares? Was I supposed to stay and fill the grave with my hands?"

"That's not the point. Since you got here, you have kept to yourself and haven't talked to people or even said Hi to some of your friends."

"I came to bury my father, not to greet people."

"These people are here for us and for dad, and you are behaving as if you've never seen them."

"Will you stop lecturing me? Thank everyone on my behalf and tell them it's over, they can leave."

"Let's pretend you never said that, and by the way, if it's the Minister you are still angry with, you better get over it. Everyone was disappointed by the . . ."

"Disappointed? I feel like getting a gun and deflating the idiot's fat stomach."

Anna looked at me bewildered. "Is that what you are learning in the States?"

"Give me a break. I'm tired."

"I thought you would not change." She left the room and

closed the door.

I turned and faced the wall, then plunged into a dreamless slumber.

Chapter 5

". . . This day a child is born unto us in the city of David, and his name shall be called Jesus . . ."

As with every Christmas, the service was held at home and attended by all the relatives who had come for the holiday. In the Christmas tradition, a pastor known to the family was invited to conduct the service, and he and his family stayed for dinner, which was served in the late afternoon. The usual congregation consisted of no less than fifteen family members with as many children as there were adults. Although no one left the farm on Christmas day, they rose early and performed their day's chores and dressed decently. The children, too, were bathed and dressed in their
newest clothes.

This time, because it was only a few days after the funeral, there were twenty eight people. I counted fifteen cousins altogether, ranging in age from three months to thirty eight years. The rest were uncles, aunties, uncles' wives, and two great aunties. The atmosphere was jovial with only a few overtones of sadness.

At 4:30 dinner was served. First the guests and senior members of the house were accommodated in the dining room, then the children, who sat on straw mats in the living room watching TV were served next. The rest of the family was scattered in bedrooms and in the courtyard, and the aunties who did the cooking ate from the hearth kitchen outside the main house. Christmas dinner was sumptuous and elaborate, and though my appetite was not at its full potential, I managed to battle through five of the eight courses that were served over the three hours that dinner lasted.

My favorite Christmas dishes were the Mpombos. These are the traditional culinary dainty for feasts and important occasions that have been passed down for hundreds of generations and mastered by only a few. The elaborate preparation of the Mpombos starts very early on the morning of the feast.

First, the expert cooks, my aunties, go to the banana garden and pick tender banana leaves which are mostly young and without a single tear.

They then carefully peel off the stems and soften the leaves further by rotating them over a hearth fire until they turn a brownish green. Old, dried banana leaves are always used in lighting the hearth fire because they help to flavor the young leaves with a delicate smoky aroma that is retained in the dish being prepared.

The main dishes, which mostly include seasoned meats, stuffed chicken, or potatoes with ground nut stew and mushrooms, are then wrapped amply and separately inside the well browned leaves and tied at the top with a thin, wet banana fiber to keep it from spilling and leaking.

Afterwards, a giant pot with some water and young banana stemmings is put on the hearth fire and the numerous wrappings put inside and covered with mature banana leaves. The cut stems and banana leaves help flavor the meats and stews, which have to cook for at least five hours.

When the Mpombos are finally served, they have the most delicate mouthwatering aroma and the memory of the savory taste remains for days.

After dinner, as the sun yellowed away, the hosts and guests in the dining room transferred to the living room where the noisy children were asked to move to Anna's room. The little ones stood up reluctantly with their swollen, little stomachs and filed into Anna's room to continue with their movies. Rather than stay in the house, I decided to take a stroll and ease the weight in my stomach.

I walked past the milking stalls towards the farm until I reached the bottom of the hill where a small river marked the edge of the farm separating it from a neighbor's plantation. I had been to the river many times as a child and not much had changed since that time. Most of the bushes had been cleared to create space for potatoes and maize, but all the trees were still standing. As kids, my cousins and I came to the river to play and bathe. The girls chose a spot upstream, refusing to bathe in water they believed to have been contaminated by the boys. We boys never objected to bathing downstream. Our secret was the big tree near the water's edge.

If you climbed onto the limb that leaned over the river, you could spot the girls bathing naked upstream. The thick bushes were closer to us so we could see the girls without them seeing us. The only problem was the limb supported just one person at a time, so we had to agree on a system where everyone took a fair peek at the bathing girls.

This remained a Christmas treat for most of my childhood. We boys were a bunch of rascals, but we could keep a secret. To this day, I'm not aware of any of the girls knowing about the mischief at the river. The vacations at the farm consisted of our giving the girls as much hell as we possibly could, which got us into a lot of trouble with the adults. Still, we returned with more mischief the following year. As the years progressed and we grew into the teens, fewer cousins came to the farm and the mischief died. Soon we became the ones policing the youngsters. Christmas at the farm was still fun, but it had changed forever.

I returned to the spot under the tree where I had liked to sit as a kid. It was a large flat rock with edges that had been smoothed by numerous feet. Many people had bathed at that spot, but not anymore because the bushes that shielded it from prying eyes had been cleared to accommodate the crops.

After sitting awhile, I heard someone walking down the footpath. The footsteps were gentle and unrushed. I assumed it was one of my aunties fetching water to be used around the house, so I remained seated, but to my surprise I saw Ellen and stood up to acknowledge her.

"Did I disturb you?" she asked.

"Oh no. Absolutely not, I was just dreaming away."

"I thought so. I knew you'd be here."

I gave her a questioning look "Am I needed at the house?"

"No. No one is looking for you. You don't mind if I join you do you?"

"Not at all."

She selected a nearby boulder and sat down.

"Did you know that your father used to come here, too?"

"Here? No."

"He liked the sound of the river. 'It makes thinking easier,' he used to say."

"I agree," I said. I found myself a little uneasy. Not only was I at a loss in conversing with her, I wasn't sure if she resented me for making no effort to be close to my father.

"You are so much like your father," she said looking at

my face. "The two of you should have been closer." Her gaze shifted from me to the water and back again. "It's good you came. We were afraid that you might not make it to the funeral."

I nodded and the silence continued, our eyes fixed on the water.

"You know your father loved you very much, don't you?" she asked at length.

"I know he did," I replied without looking up. "I regret being such a disappointment to him."

"What do you mean?" she inquired "He was so proud of you. He always talked about you."

I regarded her with that look that says, "Don't patronize me."

"I need to know if I was a disappointment to my father or if he was angry with me for some reason." My eyes were full of fear and tears. "Please be honest."

Her eyes remained locked with mine, then she dug into the pocket of her sweater and took out a thin envelope.

"He asked me to make sure you get this."

I saw the envelope and started shivering.

"He wrote it two days before he died. I was not sure when to give it you." She handed me the thin envelope. There was no name on it. Slowly I unsealed it and removed the letter inside. It was my father's handwriting. I could recognize it among a million others. The letter was short and undated.

Forgive me son if I have failed you or your sister. I tried my best as far as a man can. Look after your sister. She is a strong woman like your mother but she needs you. I look forward to meeting your mother, I will tell her how the two of you gave me pride and strength over the years.   - Papa.

My silent tears suddenly turned to uncontrollable sobs, and I shook so fiercely that Ellen had to hold me. Together we cried for a long time, and when my trembling was under control, we sat again and watched the river, sobbing silently.

"Why didn't anyone tell me he was dying?"

"Your father was a very proud man, Sim, down to the last minute. He made all of us promise not to tell you because you'd return home immediately."

"And what is wrong with that? He was my father."

"He said you seeing him in that state would devastate him more than the illness."

The sound of the river was soothing. It washed away our painful thoughts, leaving only sweet memories. A while later I broke the silence.

"What are you going to do now that he is gone?"

"I'm not yet sure, but I will be fine." She wiped tears from her face. "Being with him inspired strength in me that I didn't know I had. For me that is the greatest gift of love."

"I'm sorry for the manner in which my family has treated you."

"Oh that's OK, dear, they were only being protective of your father. He was a treasure you know, a gem to all of us," She wiped away tears again and asked when my school term commenced.

"First week of January," I said. "I'll go back to the States next week."

The image of Seattle's cold and wet streets flashed through my mind. In a few days, I would be surrounded by umbrellas and overcoats, dashing from building to building for lectures. The only comforting thought was of Romina waiting for me.

As it got darker, we walked back towards the house. I went into the hearth kitchen where I chatted with my aunties. My eyes were still red from crying, but so were theirs. We talked about many things laughing and joking. At dusk, I saw one of my cousins and Isingoma, the farmhand, leave the compound and head towards the village square. I quickly excused myself from the kitchen and joined them. After staying home almost a week without going anywhere, I was restless, yet I did not want to go visiting or to the sports club in the city where many of my friends hung out.

I wanted to stay on in the village but do something for a change. So when my cousin told me they were going to the small trading center in the village to catch the happy hour, I offered to join them. The walk to the village square took almost thirty minutes, so it was dark when we arrived.

The trading center, however, was partly illuminated. The sound of drums and excitement greeted us from half a mile away.

Isingoma led my cousin and me to a fairly large, rectangular hut detached from the main buildings of the square. The hut was lit by two kerosene lamps suspended from the middle of the roof and was semi-crowded with people sitting in small drinking clusters and talking noisily. Isingoma immediately located his friends, the gravediggers, whom we joined in the far corner of the hut. The air smelled of sweat and Waragi, a local undistilled gin. People were seated on low wooden benches arranged around small square tables on which the drinks rested. The group that we joined consisted of six men. I recognized three as the ones who had dug my father's grave. Isingoma introduced me formally, and they greeted me in turns with strong handshakes, each expressing his condolences and imparting a few words of wisdom.

"An oak does not grow in isolation young man," one

man said. "Where one has grown, another exists. Your father was the oak in this village and we shall miss him immensely.

However, we are comforted to know that we have another oak in his offspring. You. Do not despair at misfortune. Remember, the strongest oak in the forest is also the one with the most scars. You have our prayers."

The man concluded his brief speech and was acknowledged by all at the table for his sagacious counsel. I said a few words in gratitude and soon the happy hour was underway.

The merriment both outside our hut and inside intensified with time. A visiting troupe was performing folk dances in the courtyard behind the main buildings. The excited crowds cheered and the drums drowned their cheers. The woman waiting on us approached and asked how much Waragi we wanted. Because I did not drink Waragi, I asked whether she had any other type of booze, but she said there was nothing else and offered to get me a soda instead.

"Just bring Pepsi." Isingoma barked at her in the local dialect. "The man has money, don't you see him? Does he look like your usual men?"

Word around the village was that I had brought a considerable amount of dollars and exchanged them, so the men demanded that the entire night be my treat.

By now, our group had expanded to include four more friends of Isingoma's. I accepted readily and they cheered me. I felt that buying them booze was the least I could do. These men had helped prepare my father's grave, and I hadn't talked to any of them at all. From the day of the funeral, they were to be given food and booze for a period of about seven days, since the exchange of money for grave digging was taboo. This was the tradition. They always collected the food at the farm from Isingoma; however, part of the agreement seemed to have been breached when it came to the issue of booze. The gravediggers would accept no money to buy booze, and Auntie Drusilla would not hear of buying booze for them, so that part of the agreement had been left unfulfilled. But they held no grudges. They were always grateful for their daily meals at the farm.

When the woman waiting on us returned with my drink, I asked her to bring Waragi and roast pork for the men. They cheered me again and barked at her to bring their orders faster than lightning. Then they lavished her with false compliments for her big eyes and wide ass. I felt sorry for the woman. She could not have been more than eighteen. She was robust with wide toes, and her body odor could be smelled from fifteen feet away.

I watched as the men in the neighboring group groped her buttocks and pulled her nylon skirt with lustful glee. They were drunk and trying to tease her, but were, in fact, molesting her. She, in turn, just smiled and pushed their hands away, seemingly enjoying the attention. I watched my company as they masticated the pork and talked between mouthfuls. My cousin, who was no less crude than the gravediggers, said something in English and repeated it for the benefit of my ears.

"It's good Christmas, yes?" It was a question for me.

"Yes it's good," I affirmed, nodding my head. It was obvious that my drunken cousin was trying to impress the rest of the group that he could communicate in English. The absurdity, though, was that in those few words, he had nearly exhausted his English vocabulary and quite possibly not impressed anyone. My cousin had grown up in a village far from the farm and in his twenty six years had never been inside of a classroom. His formal education was limited to mediocre carpentry skills and a very good knowledge of animal husbandry. He had learned these trades through apprenticeship in his home village.

The conversations at all tables became rowdy as the night deepened. The men discussed women and used obscene language, accusing each other of sleeping with young village girls. The combined laughter and noise from the hut occasionally drowned out the noise from outside. At first, I felt uneasy wondering what I was doing in such company anyway. This was a different world altogether, a world so alien to my own that I could not possibly establish an effective wavelength on which to communicate with its inhabitants. I studied the people around me more intently.

Two of the groups in the hut included women. The women were no different from their male counterparts. They hurled obscenities at anyone and laughed them off. Many of the people in the hut had peeling lips from the consumption of too much crude Waragi. Even their sweat smelled of it. Most of them wore thick rubber sandals made from truck tires, and their clothes, which were dirty and torn at the shoulders, didn't reflect much Christmas spirit. I thought how two weeks earlier I could never have imagined that I would spend Christmas night several thousand miles away in a village hut with drunken gravediggers. I probably would have expected to be in some night club partying away amidst loud music and sweaty bodies as I had done the previous year. How similar the two nights were, and yet how different.

I looked at the men and listened to their conversations and smiled wryly. They were mostly drifters from distant villages, and all that mattered to them was their food and booze. I wondered how they would react if I told them the Waragi they drank could rupture their spleens and kill them. They would probably shrug me off because they had lived this kind of life all their years. They were comfortable in their ignorance, and I was uncertain of my meager knowledge.

With time, they tried to involve me in their conversations. They wanted me to tell them about white people and their country. They had strange theories and stories about white women, but when I dismissed them as false, I detected disappointment on their faces. They were hungry for nice, juicy stories from the strange land and customs of America. They told me they wouldn't booze again for the next few days because it was time for their quarterly hunt.

First, they would consult with an oracle from a neighboring village and, in two days, they would set out for the Forest of the Snake. When that time came, they would carry spears, machetes, and nets, and disappear from the village for several days.

Sometimes not all of them returned. They told me of occasions when they lost friends in the forest. Some were killed by beasts and others simply vanished. To survive the forest, they had to be sober. Each wore a special charm around his neck and, because of superstition, never talked to any women on the day the hunt began.

It was rumored in the nine villages surrounding the forest that many years ago a young, very beautiful virgin from one of the villages conceived through mystic powers. Months later, in the throes of labor, she gave birth to a two-headed python which slithered off and disappeared in the forest. To find her child, the girl isolated herself from society and went to search in the forest.

At night, she sang to her child to come back to her and, the more she sang, the thicker the forest grew. Soon, it swallowed four of the nine villages and became so big that hunters took more than five days to reach its center, which was devoid of trees. It was also said by those who knew, that the girl herself had turned into a beautiful snake, and that if you stood by the edge of the forest on the night of every third moon and honed your ears, you heard a sweet lullaby coming from the forest.

The words of the song were in a strange language, but they reminded everyone who heard them of enduring maternal love. In fact, valiant hunters who had ventured to the center of the forest spoke of the most beautiful snake that the human eye ever beheld. In the middle of the night at full moon, the snake climbed onto a rock that sat in the middle of the forest. The colors of her skin were phenomenal. Her poise upon the rock, regal. When she began to sing, you fell on your knees and held out your hands in sacrificial abandon. The melody was so sweet, the voice so gentle, so tender and so perfectly indescribable. At that moment, you were transported out of this world and became one with eternity, but only for the midnight hour.

Soon, she stopped singing and disappeared back into the forest leaving you with a great sense of rejuvenation. Only three hunters had ever returned to tell of this story. They hailed from different villages and had lived several generations apart, but each of them had lived in good health for almost two hundred years. The Forest of the Snake was every hunter's creed. Many men had vanished there, never to return. Some died before getting even halfway to the center, and others died on the return after having failed to reach the center. When the hunters returned, they were often changed men, highly regarded in the villages. However, the drunkards returned with only stories. They never commanded much respect and, with time, they drowned themselves in Waragi again and counted three full moons before the next trip.

By now, I was intoxicated by their world. They were so real that I wanted to be like them for one moment. To know only superstition and charm, to worship the hunt, to drift through life unburdened by information, to be down to earth without pretensions of transcendent values. It struck me oddly that where millions around the world were celebrating the birth of a savior, these men celebrated yet a different kind of salvation. For them, Christianity was a fallacy. There cannot be only one truth and only one way to find it.

Here was a salvation in the snake—the same snake that saved the children of Israel from perishing in the wilderness—the snake of the forest. For them, the forest was the altar and their lives were the sacrifice. They cleansed themselves quarterly and pilgrimaged to the middle of the forest to breathe salvation and to reconcile with eternity. How could anyone seek to invalidate such faith as a truth? To say it lacks a way and a life? What amount of malice or bigotry could one carry around in his heart to proclaim such injustices?

I told them stories about the strange land and they listened with awe. My imagination fascinated me and I rejoiced in its power. I fabricated stories about that strange place, gesturing powerfully, now raising my voice, then lowering it. I held their gazes and hypnotized them until they were lost in a stupor. I told them stories about American women and how they would rush to seduce the gravediggers should they ever set foot in that strange land. What they would do to them in styles the men had never imagined. They quivered. I knew I had them in a grip.

The drumming from outside was enchanting and the aura inside the dimly lit hut became magical.

I was now in their primitive world.

This is what they want to hear, it's what they thrive on. Feed it to them by the baskets, be generous, it's Christmas.

I felt like Jesus on the mount, feeding my unblinking listeners shit. They ate the shit and washed it down with crude Waragi. In my heart, I felt justified. *On this day, oh Son of David, I am blameless and I commit no sin, for I only give where I am asked. This is their happy hour. I give them what they want. Some of them shall not return from that forest.*

. . . when the sons of God return to present themselves before the Lord and Satan comes among them, the Lord shall say to Satan: "Whence have you come?"

And Satan shall answer: "From going to and fro on the earth, and from walking up and down on it."

Then the Lord shall say: "Have you considered my servant Sim, that there is none as devious as he, a dishonest and immoral man who feeds men shit when they ask for it and watches them wash it down with crude Waragi?"

And Satan shall say: "Does he do so for naught? Hast thou not made his life full of shit?"

Chapter 6

My apartment was clean and smelled fresh when I returned to Seattle. A bunch of mail was neatly stacked on the kitchen counter, and there was a small Christmas tree near the TV with a beautifully wrapped medium sized box under it. Before leaving for Uganda, I had left Romina copies of my apartment and mailbox keys. I had no idea she would clean up the place and decorate it for Christmas. Upon arriving at the airport, I had been tempted to call her, but then decided to wait until I got home. The shuttle from the airport took forty five minutes, and when I reached home, I was reluctant to wake her since it was late. I knew she would be up early preparing for work and decided it would be best to call her at work.

I looked through the mail quickly and separated out the bills for which I immediately wrote checks. However, what caught my eye and excited me was the application package from Stanford University. I read it from front to back and examined the application forms, going over every last detail. I would have to write four essays in all, which was no problem for me. Faculty recommendations were no object either as I was friends with most of my professors, and they thought highly of me.

The only nagging issue was the awfully high figure for tuition and the fact that financial aid for foreign students was nearly non-existent. I was sure that asking for aid would jeopardize my chances for admission. So, to compete effectively with thousands of capable applicants, I would have to forego financial aid on my application. My father had put aside some money for our schooling, but I was sure my share of it would barely cover one year at Stanford.

My only solution would be to work for Malik again until I saved enough money to cover at least one year's fees.

With the money put aside by my father and what I had in the bank, I would have to deliver Malik's merchandise for about twelve weeks to raise enough money to cover school for one year.

Whereas this amounted to betraying my own will and the unspoken promise to Romina, I thought it was the most practical solution. I reread the Stanford brochure with dreamy relish, seeing with every page visions of myself as a student strolling through the campus's splendidly manicured quadrangles and embracing the autumn sunset as it cast golden shadows on the yellowing leaves.

I imagined myself as one of several students walking briskly to lectures, very promising and proud and mingling freely with some of the sharpest minds of the century.

There was no end in sight to the possibilities. I simply had to be there, to be one of them and make my father proud in his grave. I was sure my application would be completed and in the mail in two weeks. However, it would be until mid-June before the university wrote back. There was obviously no hurry. I needed the time to line up my cards.

School began early on a Tuesday. In the four days since returning, I had not phoned Romina or anybody else. No one knew I was back except my 70 year old neighbor whom I met in the elevator. In fact, she too had no idea I was away, having recently returned from Christmas vacation herself.

I spent much of the first two days in the bookstore lining up with hundreds of other students to buy the books required for winter quarter. Afterwards, my days became bleak and unbearable. I tried to rent movies in the evenings, but almost always failed to complete viewing them. Even watching TV required effort. Mostly, I sat on the carpet and huddled against the sofa with my head over my knees. Battered by unknown demons, I spent every evening in this position until darkness fell. I was even afraid to turn on the lights or make a phone call. When my back became numb, I would stroll to the bedroom and flop onto the bed until morning when the alarm summoned me into yet another of my severely depressed days.

No matter how dejected I felt, I resolved to work even harder on my academics. My grades were not to suffer in any manner because gaining admission to Stanford was the sole motivating force in my life. I knew that in September my chains would come undone when I strolled onto the Stanford campus as a student. That dream was not to be compromised.

On the second Tuesday of school, I returned home at three in the afternoon and, as usual, dove right into homework at the kitchen table. When darkness fell, I resumed my position at the foot of the sofa. I was by now accustomed to this routine and was getting comfortable with it. It was like a state of spiritual meditation, blanking out my mind and cleansing it of thought and fear.

I had been seated for an hour when I heard a noise at the door. Before I knew what was going on, Romina entered the apartment and switched on the hall light. When she saw me, a whimper escaped her and she almost ran out of the apartment, thinking I was an intruder. Then she turned on the living room light, her face full of shock. Realizing how awkward the scene must be, I stood up and said her name softly as if to assuage her fear.

"Are you OK, Sim?" she asked impulsively. "You scared me. What are you doing here like this?"

"I'm OK. I'm fine," I tried to reassure her.

"Why are the lights off?"

"I kinda forgot about them. I was thinking about other stuff." I moved closer and touched her shoulder reassuringly "I'm really OK."

"When did you get back?"

"A few days ago." I watched her face for any change in emotion, but she continued studying me for reassurance.

"Are you really fine?" she asked again.

"I'm OK, really."

"You have lost weight," she said touching my face gently. "Haven't you been eating?" She went into the kitchen and looked in the fridge. There was a can of soft spread and old sliced cheese. A half loaf of bread sat on the kitchen counter next to a tin of peanut butter, and the sink was littered with used tea bags.

"Bread and tea?" she asked with a sarcastic chuckle. "Are you trying to starve yourself?"

Wordlessly, I looked at her, a broad smile covering my face. I felt warm inside. My sweet Romina was back.

"What's funny?"

"I'm just happy to see you again. I'm really sorry I did not call. But I've been feeling really crappy and wouldn't have been much company."

"That's OK. You'll be fine." We held each other and kissed.

"You almost gave me a heart attack."

"I'm sorry. I will never scare you like that again."

"Promise?"

"Promise."

She asked me about my family and how they were handling my father's loss.

"They saw it coming for months so their grief has not been overwhelming."

"How about you?" she asked. "You had no idea."

"Well, it will pass, I guess."

"I'm really sorry." She kissed me once more and surveyed the kitchen again with disbelief. "You can't live on bread alone you know."

"I think I'm doing just fine," I laughed.

"It's not funny. Let's go and get some groceries. I need to fatten you up."

"That sounds good." I picked up the jacket she had bought me for Christmas and thanked her for it.

"Do you like it?"

"Of course. I love it." It was made of warm distressed leather, handcrafted in Honduras. "Perfect. Just perfect," I said.

After spending a few days with Romina, my spirits improved. I called Malik and resumed my old job ferrying boxes of merchandise from the hangar to the houseboat on Lake Union. Malik asked about my family's wellbeing and counseled me to be strong. Mario, who had taken over my responsibilities, was glad to be back at the boathouse concentrating solely on the distribution of the product and watching the last few games of the football season.

On my first trip to the boathouse, I was met by Mario at the boardwalk that led from the road to the boats. He was now spotting a second gold tooth in the lower jaw and was obviously rushed. He told me immediately that he had changed his bet once again. This time he was sure the Cowboys would retain the championship. I thought I had interrupted him watching a game. Together, we quickly moved the boxes from the van to the house where he immediately commenced verifying the contents.

When I went to the bathroom, I discovered why he was in such a hurry. On the cabinet next to the bathroom sink was a woman's wristwatch and next to it a thin makeup kit. On the smooth side of the kit was a powdery substance that had been cut up into four thin lines using a laminated card lying nearby. It was obvious now that I had interrupted no football game but rather a pleasure trip. No wonder his bedroom was closed, too—a rare occurrence.

Recognizing this as a good opportunity to satisfy my curiosity, I poured two of the powder portions on the makeup kit into the toilet before flushing, then rejoined Mario who was still verifying the shipment.

"Aahhh, that's some really, really strong stuff," I said, rubbing my nose fiercely to appear as if I had snorted some of it. "I did a couple of lines. I hope you don't mind."

"It's OK. I got plenty."

"Aren't you worried about Torres finding out that you are using his stuff?"

"Nooo, Torres ma man. Look at that." He pointed to three boxes in the corner of the room. "That's surplus." He told me Torres was frequently flying in more than the usual two hundred pounds of product and now two or three boxes remained after Gemma's men took their share. Malik was looking for ways to dispense with the surplus since it was safer to have the entire product gone as soon as possible.

"Ma man gave me that himself," he said, pointing towards the bathroom. "I only use it for fun. You know."

Now I had my confirmation.

"You know what?" Mario said, seemingly frustrated from counting the endless bags inside the boxes. "I trust you man. I know everything is there." He shoved all the boxes into the corner, including those he hadn't verified yet. "I got a gringa waiting, bro, if you know what I mean."

"I know, dude. You go have fun." I took my cash and left.

Now that I knew of the surplus, an idea I had toyed with earlier returned and set my thoughts racing. It was a brilliant one, I thought, but it involved approaching Malik with a bold proposal that required me to stick my head deeper into the operation than I already had. Still, I toyed with the idea but remained reluctant to go ahead with it.

The ending days of the month had been unusually pleasant with the sun occasionally peeking through the clouds and people strolling outside. It was winter, though, and temperatures were still low. The college application had been completed and mailed in January and now I concentrated on academics.

Occasionally, I talked to Anna at Aisha's home, and if she was not available, I left a message. She was now nearing the middle of her third trimester and said she was as swollen as a balloon. I sent her money occasionally although she insisted that I needed it more than she did. She was at home after all, I was the one thousands of miles away. She encouraged me to save it for a rainy day, and so I did.

The fax from Uganda was a seven page document from the family lawyers in Kampala detailing the matter of a debt owed to the bank by my father who had taken out two big loans. Part of the money had been put into our college funds, but the remainder, the bigger portion, had gone towards our father's treatment, which, of course, was like attempting to fill a bottomless pit. The money had not been fully repaid by the time he died. So in an effort to recover the balance, the bank was going after the family estate, particularly the three hundred acres of farmland in Gayaza where the family home was situated.

For two months, the lawyers had taken up arms against the bank and secured an injunction against its actions which had now been overturned by a superior court. Their subsequent efforts to save the estate were in vain, and the final ruling was for the estate of the deceased to pay the entire fifty three thousand dollars including interest within ninety days from the first day of March. Failure to do so would result in transfer of the estate's ownership to the bank.

My reaction to this news was immediate denial. I refused to let the depth of its implications hit me.

This could not be happening. It had to be a joke of some kind or some mistake. What I had just read was merely ink stains on a piece of paper, how could they have the power to transform my world?

I walked to the kitchen and fixed myself some tea and a peanut butter sandwich. After eating, I returned to the sofa and reread the fax. In the recesses of my mind, alarms were going off as it slowly sank in that this was real and not a joke or mistake. I sat a long time in the darkness staring at the wall opposite me until it ceased to be visible. By night fall, I was back at the foot of the sofa huddled over my knees.

If the bank took over the estate, they would level it and transform the entire three hundred acres into a coffee plantation. That was their style. They had done it to many families without compromise or mercy. They gave you thirty days to vacate and never allowed the family to harvest the crops or sell any of the animals, reasoning that everything on the land was part of the estate. All you took away were your personal effects and the furniture. Because I was my father's heir and the estate had been transferred into my name when he died, it was my foremost duty to keep the family together as my father had done. Losing the farm would devastate them. The lawyers were merely instruments to be used by me in effecting my duties.

I was terrified by the thought of my family being forced off the farm. Anna would probably find an apartment in the city and live there with granny and Auntie Drusilla. The rest of the family would have to fend for themselves. How could I let such an injustice happen to them, and how could I possibly justify it?

My sister was pregnant and due in a matter of weeks, and I had promised my dead father to take care of her and her baby. The child would need a home to grow up in and play from, not the miserable corridors of an apartment building. He needed to chase squirrels, milk cows, and weed crops. He needed to bathe in the river and run through the plantation with his cousins. It had been like that for generations and was supposed to remain that way. I not only owed it to my children and their children, I was bound by my ancestors to maintain tradition as they had done.

I had been selected after all before I was conceived in my mother's womb, to be the first son and, therefore, the watcher over the family when my father passed on. My time had now come. To betray that ancestral trust was unheard of. Failing to protect the family from predators was probably excusable, but what ate me up was the fact that thirteen generations of my family were buried on that very land with my father having joined them only a few weeks earlier. These were their resting grounds, the spiritual abode without which they ceased to exist.

The looming horror was that in three months' time, graders and tractors could flatten the land and replace my family's ancestral roots with a coffee plantation. As watcher, it was my duty to protect these grounds without excuse, for in the spiritual world there is no listening to reason. One was either weak and incompetent or chivalrous and worthy of their mandate.

As first child, I had the ancestral mandate. To betray it by allowing the farm to be turned into coffee beans for high strung Europeans was enough for me to be cursed a million-fold by each individually and by all collectively. My blood would be tainted by that curse, blemishing all who descended from me with unspeakable misfortune. I had witnessed with my own eyes what an ancestral curse meant, and I'd rather die than endure its consequences.

The following day, I was startled by the alarm. I hit the off button and resumed my slumber. I had slept very little that night and was in no condition to go to school and certainly in no mood for Professor Stein's group discussions in sociology class.

At noon, I left bed and took a long shower, then had some coffee and a couple of eggs. The week had dragged on for an eternity, but Friday was refreshingly crisp and clear so I decided to take a walk. I needed to unbend my leaden mind so I could think clearly.

I examined the random direction of my life, wondering whether it was predetermined the day I was born or whether I was capable of steering and influencing it. All I wanted was a degree from a good school followed by a career in business, but life kept boxing me in, delivering one tragedy after another. Why did it have to be so hard?

At an intersection, I turned left into a neighborhood I had never seen before. The road narrowed and curved around a wooded hillside dead ending two hundred yards ahead. A few meters to my left was a small, fenced memorial park. The marble gravestones were laid in even rows amidst towering evergreens and a well-tended lawn. I selected a cluster of evergreens just outside the gate and sat in their shade.

From the time I was twelve, I knew I was heir to my father. For a long time that carried no deeper meaning for me than a fancy way of saying I was an only son. That had changed. Being suddenly flung into a position of making decisions that were my father's was very scary.

I had no training or background in these issues at all. But such was life, I told myself. All one had to do was make the best of it without being a disappointment. I felt as if I was running a relay that spanned generations—the kind where you are unexpectedly handed a baton and must run without knowing when to pass it on. All you can do is run as best as you can. My great grandfathers had run in that race, passing down the baton to my grandfather who, in turn, passed it to my father and, now, it was in my hand.

When my grandfather died, I was very young and was, at the time, convinced of the existence of a giant hole in which people fell never to return. My grandfather had been like a wall standing between the family and that hole, but it had swallowed him and he was never seen again. My father had become the new wall and he was now gone.

I could not kid myself in interpreting the symbolism that had persisted for generations: to be heir was to be the unprotected protector when your time came. So, with every passing moment, I saw the space between me and the abyss grow smaller and smaller.

I wished to reverse everything and return to a childhood filled with innocence, but that was a sweet era gone and could only exist in dreams, a luxury I could afford no more. I had to find a way of raising almost sixty thousand dollars in less than sixty days, and no amount of innocence or dreaming would be useful in achieving such a task.

While sitting up all night, I had finally made the decision that selling the surplus drugs at the houseboat was the best way to go. I would be able to raise a lot of money in a very short time and who knows how much I could save in ninety days. The apparent lack of wisdom in this decision is what weighed me down. It was definitely doable but would I be stupid enough to go through with it? At the moment, there seemed no viable alternative.

I stood up and strode back towards the street. Inside the cemetery near the small gate, an elderly couple laid a beautiful wreath on a marble grave. The woman was frail and her left hand shook atop a walking stick. Her right hand was hooked into the arm of the gentleman whom I assumed to be her husband.

He was of equally delicate countenance and wore a brown beret and an old cotton jacket. They exchanged a few words and guided each other along the narrow asphalt path, their wrinkled faces expressive of distance and experience. I wondered what their story was and how dramatic it must be if they told it. Would the benefit of its years provide some wisdom for a troubled youth whose life was at a crossroads?

Earlier I had considered approaching Malik and relating my story with the probability that he might loan me the money and allow me to work off the debt in some manner, but that was farfetched and wishful. If Malik sensed any desperation on my part, he would terminate me from the operation, severely damaging my chances.

To execute my plan successfully, I had to take care of two issues. First, my plan of selling off the surplus had to be solidified, which meant talking to my friend Junkichi about a plan we had sketched earlier in the quarter. I would see him on Monday after class. Second, I had to convince Malik that I could do an effective job dispensing the drugs without inviting any problems. That, I might have to put an effort into, but I was hopeful. I would wait until Monday to start the ball rolling. If I rested my mind first, perhaps I would be in a better position to tackle my problems.

I called Romina as soon as I arrived at the apartment and begged her to ask for Saturday off in the hope of spending all weekend with her. Her company was like therapy, and I found myself wanting to spend more time with her. Though she never cured my deepening sense of foreboding, her presence and charm numbed it and allowed me to connect with another human being.

In his memoirs, psychologist C.G. Jung wrote that loneliness does not derive from having no people about oneself but from being unable to communicate the things that one considers important or from holding certain views that others find inadmissible.

Such was my quandary. Very often, I wanted to share my inner thoughts with Romina and, in so doing, invite her into my lonesome world, but I always hesitated, thinking her reaction to my problems might be merely conceptual, and she might recognize only what drove my fears without actually understanding the depth of my dilemma. She was, after all, from a very different cultural background than mine.

For me to think she would understand my apprehensive reaction to ancestral expectations would be overly presumptuous. I was convinced that she would not accept my selling drugs as justification to save my family, so I never shared my deeper troubles fearing that they might poison the relationship by burdening her and pushing her away.

After leaving work that afternoon, Romina went to a friend's house to do her hair. I picked her up at seven and was awed by how radiant she looked. She seemed to achieve this with little effort, like a master painter producing a wholly different masterpiece every time she changed her hairstyle.

We drove to Central Market in Lynnwood for fresh produce and her favorite spices and then swung by the little video store near her place to rent a couple of videos. At night, she prepared a scrumptious dinner of avocado gratin filled with salmon bits, garlic, mushrooms, and Oaxaca cheese. Her place was a two bedroom condo she had bought on the second floor of a three story building in the Northgate area. The bedrooms were tiny and faced the street, but the living room was uncharacteristically large with huge sliding doors facing westward with a partial view of the Olympic Mountains.

She had several plants in the living room as it received plenty of natural light. Summer sunsets from here were incredible as the sun fell behind the mountains unobstructed by neighboring buildings.

Her bedroom was almost entirely occupied by her bed, a burgundy divan covered in throws and an intrusively large chiffonier made from solid mahogany. The second room was her miscellaneous room. In it she had a crammed bookshelf, a computer that sat on a low stool in the corner, and a laundry basket next to a cushion chaise that she converted into a bed when friends stayed over. The living room was full of native South American art, mostly collected from her days in the Peace Corps. The centerpiece was a richly textured Peruvian weaving about three feet long that she had brought back from Iquitos.

If there was one decorating talent Romina had, it was an eye for earthy tones and soft hues. Her whole place was done up in soft yellows and delicate pastels with upholstery to match. She had painted each room herself in different colors and had torn out the living room carpet replacing it with hard woods. At night, the lighting was softly filtered through artsy lamp shades placed around the room.

Because she had no dining table, we normally ate from the sofa in front of the TV. This time she laid out a sleeping bag on the floor which we sat on, eating stuffed avocado and sipping three day old organic syrah served in coffee mugs.

After dinner, we cruised downtown to one of my favorite dives, an African club called Gray Savannah. We drank, danced, and drank more. On the dance floor, we necked like high school kids ruled by impulse and driven to reckless abandon in a conspiracy between the sweet booze and the sly DJ.

Gray Savannah was not a fancy, big budget club. Its main draw was the DJ who boasted a large following of African and Caribbean music lovers. Situated in the downtown area, the club's main entrance was in the alley between First and Second Avenues and manned by two humongous Kenyans. If you loved Congolese Rumba, Soukous, Reggae, or East Indies' Zouk, this was the place to be every Friday night. I absolutely loved this club, so much so that it's the only place Romina ever saw me dancing. She, too, loved it but she was more of a free spirit and danced with ease to a lot of different types of music while I was quite inhibited. This was the only place I could get myself to dawdle around on the dance floor and remain oblivious of my surroundings. Here the music flowed in idyllic strings which evoked a primordial response that defied sitting down.

By midnight, the club was jamming. The boozers were drunk and the dancers sweating as the melodious rhythms of the tom-toms and marimbas engulfed the club. Romina and I lost ourselves among the other revelers, drowning in rivers of sweat, bulbous bosoms, and soft waists. This was Gray Savannah, a heaving jungle of momentary enchantment and intoxicating languor.

. . . In the jungle, I beheld a bewitchingly beauteous princess, her hair a ravenous mane. Her eyes were covered by a narrow silver mask and her gown woven in delicate rainbow thread. She touched me softly and whispered sweet hypnotizing words, then opened the gates to her dominion and bid me along a forest path covered in morning dew and profuse with the sweet smell of river hyacinths. With a pounding heart and throbbing will, I traveled down the forest path to the center of her world, her innermost universe. It was lush and covered with begonias and geraniums. Together we danced the moon dance, bathed in incandescent light and surrounded by forest lilies. This was now my world—my release from pain, for I, Simon Peter Wasswa, omnipotent prince from Luwero to Mubende and even Kasensero in Kyotera, had found redemption in her world.

We left Gray Savannah in the wee hours and drove east towards the freeway and then northward to Romina's place. As I was utterly drunk, she took the wheel, allowing me to lie back in the passenger seat and watch the street lights turn the short ride north into a cosmic trip of shooting stars and peculiar sounds.

We pounced at each other the moment her door was secured. Kissing and fumbling, we made it to the bedroom where I removed her clothes and wrestled with my own. On the bed, I kneaded her breasts and sucked the large protuberant nipples. Her chest heaved against mine, her breath warm and shivering with passion. I grabbed handfuls of her hair, kissed her sweaty neck, sucked her quivering lips then her naked breasts and continued in gentle circles on her stomach downward into the moist softness of her pubis. She gasped for breath and gently rocked her hips while rubbing my face between her legs, and then pulled me up towards her. With unbridled voracity, I pushed her parted knees against her chest and watched blood rush to her face as her entire being transformed into a primordial instinct under my weight.

Drunk and weighed down by grief and lust, I was lost in this moment. The thighs and breasts invited abandon and the gyrating hips promised release. My salvation was the flesh, drawing me savagely towards an elusive Eden abounding with pleasure and lacking pain. I wanted to live in that moment forever, to forget myself in its oblivion and cast my burdens to its sweet intensity, but it rushed by like a river, too supple to be harnessed, and too delicate to be polluted by my burden. It was her moment now, one of pure love and passion, untainted by false hopes. I rocked her tenderly and felt her shiver, then consumed in a pleasure vortex she kicked her legs out and grabbed onto the headboard as I drove her feverishly to a sublime climax.

Romina was truly my first love. I could talk about my high school coming of age relationships as my first love experiences, but I'd be debasing what I experienced with Romina.

In a period of six months, what started as a mutual infatuation evolved into a highly passionate affair in which my world was transformed from a pedestrian frat boy image of love to a sobering, emotional roller coaster that took us through two years of incredible passion and periods of maddening anxiety. In that period, we broke up no less than four times but never stayed apart longer than three weeks. Romina was very kind, very passionate, very sexual, and incredibly sexy. She loved animals, did not eat meat except for fish, voted dutifully, and never preached to me.

Unfortunately, she was excessively insecure. She never ceased to think she was overweight and was horrified of growing bald. Seeing her hair in the shower drain drove her crazy. Also the fact that we were mismatched by age fanned her insecurities. On several occasions, she mentioned her concern about my swimming in a sea of young, beautiful girls on campus while she slaved away at work.

In many ways, I did not help alleviate that insecurity. Initially, I was fixated with maintaining some distance and mystique thinking it afforded me some advantage in the relationship. My attitude did a lot to create anxieties, and she kicked me out of her place a few times never wanting to see me again, but, somehow, I always endeared myself back to her. I could not be without her and our brief separations devastated me.

It's a mystery why people love, and I never really understood why Romina loved me. It obviously had nothing to do with the bullshit stories I told her about myself, or the physical aspect of our relationship, for, although we were very dynamic lovers, that alone could not have had the power to propel a two year relationship all by itself.

Suffering my own insecurities, I sought to color up my life by fabricating stories about my childhood in Uganda. She was, after all, the political activist sort that idolized Che Guevara and had spent three years in the Peace Corps in Latin America, helping the unprivileged, something I could never do. While I grew up in a poor country, my family was anything but poor.

We were never part of the $40 a month statistic. I had an American-like, middle class upbringing in a third world country, and my dreams were Ivy League and international business. But she was different. She was passionate about the wellbeing of others, about the outdoors life, and the environment. I did not care much about that stuff. When I looked at myself through her eyes, I found myself to be extremely shallow and soulless. I had no deep rooted political convictions. I liked big cars and McDonalds. I had come to America to live a dream of abundance, not minimalism.

Yet, here was this incredible woman who loved me. She opened my eyes and showed me this alien world of selflessness that I had never seen, and my first impulse was a fear of losing her because my life had no depth. Naturally, I manufactured depth and mystique.

I became this person who had endured a very hard childhood, whose family had been brutalized and almost annihilated for political reasons. I told her about endless days of hunger and weeklong treks on foot fleeing persecutors.

That I had come out of this kind of childhood undamaged and now enjoyed a reasonably normal life was amazing to her.

My Romina believed all this. How could someone so nurturing and big hearted not believe it? Her life was an open book to me and mine was just a long tale. She knew no Ugandans to verify my story, and, even if she had, what would they say? This was the reality of a Ugandan life, except it was not my reality. All the stories I told her were real, but they were not my own. It was much easier for me to be a pathetic liar than a truthful loser.

I could not dare be truthful. Whereas it's true that I had some bad childhood moments, they were limited to the disappearance of my mother and the deaths of a few close relatives. However, in a country endemic with poverty, pestilence, and ruthless dictators, this was the only suffering I had known. My bourgeois upbringing far outweighed my suffering credentials. This was the soft underbelly of my life—in a country with a mere eight digit gross domestic product, my family shopped in Europe and owned a three hundred acre ranch. Could she know this and not laugh me right out of her life, my Che loving Romina?

Chapter 7

Junkichi Yoshimura, known as Jun, was a Japanese foreign student who started attending the University of Washington at the same time I did. He, too, was majoring in international business, and, over the months, he and I took several classes together and became close friends. Even with a characteristic flair that bordered on flamboyance, Jun was very outgoing and likeable. Like me, he was a member of the Foreign Students' Association and my haze buddy when we joined the PKK fraternity.

Whereas PKK's members were some of the brightest students on campus, it also had a collection of wild party goers who gave the campus's party frats a run for their money by throwing wild parties that almost always ended with police intervention and minor arrests. In the spirit of indulgence, Jun and I never missed these parties where blending the endless booze with willing girls and the occasional pharmaceutical was customary. When PKK partiers wearied of the police busting in on their parties, they started organizing them more discreetly and called them underground gigs.

These were held off campus in locations as varied as the Industrial District and the docks at Fisherman's Terminal. These gigs attracted the wildest partygoers on campus and were notorious for having only hard liquor, drugs, and mineral water as refreshments. Even the water came at a high markup for those whose blood needed a little dilution. It was at one of these gigs that I learned of Jun's secret enterprise in MDMA and Ice. Jun had contrived a clever dispensation mechanism using rigged beer cans that had false bottoms and top buttons that released individual gel tabs when pressed. The cans easily held over a hundred tabs.

When you saw Jun at one of the gigs, he looked like any other guy having fun. But if you were an insider, you knew that the Budweiser cans he held were loaded with tablets of crystal meth, and the Heinekens contained the more popular MDMA, commonly referred to as Ecstasy or simply X. Jun's X was reputed to be the purest, and it sold for as high as thirty dollars a hit, one hit containing 1/16 of a gram of the potent powder. At these gigs, he easily sold up to five cans of X and at least three of Ice. He never told me directly how or where he got the drugs, but over the months and several gigs later, I learned that his family was in the business.

When the idea of selling Malik's surplus drugs first popped into my head, Jun was the first person I thought of. I knew he could come up with some practical ideas on how to deal off the eighty or so pounds of surplus cocaine at the houseboat, and I had mentioned it to him in passing. So, one morning at the cafeteria, I brought it up again.

"Do you remember the boxes of cocaine I talked to you about last month?"

"Yes?"

"I'm thinking about selling the stuff myself. I'm sure I can make a killing on the profits."

"How are you going to do it?"

"That's where you come in."

My voice was deliberately low to keep students at neighboring tables from overhearing.

"You said there was a couple of ways it could be done. We would split the profit, you know."

"I can probably hook you up with someone, but I can't personally get involved with the deal."

"Why not?"

"I just can't."

"Hey, we're not talking about tons of stuff here. Besides, you're already connected in the retail section."

"Not for coke. If I'm even mistakenly thought to be getting into coke my people might get uncalled for repercussions. I don't want to be the one responsible for that."

By "my people" Jun was talking about his extended family, which he had told me earlier claimed were descendants from the fifteenth century Daimyo of Miyamoto Hata, warrior and chieftain in feudal Japan and founder of what is probably the largest and most powerful of the Yakuza clans. Naturally, Jun never associated his family with Yakuza in any way, and the word itself never came up between us. However, Miyamoto Hata is a well-documented name in Japanese history, which made it rather easy to connect the dots between Jun's lineage and some of his family's dealings that I was aware of.

The Yakuza clans are known for their loyalty and honor amongst themselves, and part of their success stems largely from the division of enterprise that they have adhered to for centuries. To avoid conflict, every clan specialized in a particular type of business, ranging from smuggling, extortion, and drugs, to counterfeiting, and assassinations. Jun's family specialized in money laundering, lobbying, and had cornered the market for synthetic drugs in the Pacific Rim region.

Their North American operation was based in Vancouver B.C. where the family owned banks, art galleries, and a racecourse. Their involvement with the drug trade was limited to MDMA and crystal meth. Drugs, such as cocaine and heroin, were claimed by other clans. To deal those drugs would be regarded as an intrusion and breach of honor. Jun's reluctance to get directly involved with cocaine was justifiably steadfast.

"What should I do now?" I asked with resignation.

"Like I said, I can hook you up with someone and settle for a one time commission."

"Really? Who?"

"I know this snowboarder dude in Portland," Jun went on. "I met him last year at the gig where the rugby guys fought. Do you remember that night?"

"Yes."

"I'm sure this guy will be interested."

"What's his name?"

"Carl."

"Have you talked to him since?"

"Of course. I've done some business with him, too."

"Can he be trusted?"

"What do you need trust for?" Jun asked humorously. "You give him the powder and he gives you the cash, that's all you need."

"You know what I mean. I don't want to deal with someone who'll pull a gun on me."

"I wouldn't even mention him if I thought he was like that."

"Well then, we should use him."

"I can organize for the two of you to meet tomorrow."

"No, don't rush it. I have to be sure that my boss will let me sell the stuff first."

"I thought you already did that."

"Not yet, I wanted to talk to you before I tell him anything."

"The ball's in your court."

After a week of repeated calls, Malik finally found time to speak with me and set an appointment at his office in Madrona. He told me he had a conference to attend that afternoon and could only see me for a short time.

As I drove from school to Madrona, my mind raced with thoughts about the meeting. Here I was, with a chance to make the pitch for my life and I had no idea where to start. What would I say to Malik? What choice of words would be most effective? I had thought the scenario over for more than a week but had changed it repeatedly until I gave up and opted for a straightforward approach. Now, that too seemed lacking. In order for Malik to allow me to sell the surplus cocaine, I would have to come up with a convincing argument. Alongside the sensitivity the issue of drugs carried, I was well aware of Malik's cynicism and reluctance to indulge other people's ambitions in his personal enterprise. This was quite evident in how rigidly he managed the office.

I was also severely handicapped by the time factor and saw no way to present my case effectively in the five or so minutes he gave me before going to the conference. I considered ditching the idea, but I had already set up the appointment and had to see it through.

"I'm sorry I couldn't see you earlier," said Malik when I walked into his office. "I've been very busy all week. Is there a problem?"

"No, there's no problem." Although the cocaine issue had never come up between us, I was not reluctant to plunge directly into the matter. Malik had, after all, left me to figure it out by myself. It was unlikely that he expected me to believe the boxes Torres flew in weekly were actually loaded with chalk or printer ink. So I reminded him of the excess product at the houseboat and told him of the rich friend I had who would willingly buy the product whenever it was available.

His first reaction was apprehension. "Have you been talking to people about this?" I quickly defused that by lying that the friend in question had no idea what I did, but occasionally confided in me about his business.

He then asked a few questions and appeared reluctant to the deal, which I had feared he would be but was, nevertheless, prepared for. I went on to tell him how this friend would buy the entire weekly surplus and was willing to work on Malik's terms regarding the prices and the nature of the transactions. I continued eloquently before Malik asked why I was interested in selling the product myself. I answered without a hint of desperation that my family had slipped into financial straits since my father's passing and I needed to help out. Also, it wouldn't hurt to have a little more money myself.

"You are doing a good job currently. Let's keep it that way."

"I would really appreciate the opportunity to help out my family."

"Let's keep it the way it is, Simon. That's my decision."

I knew nothing would change that decision and did not bother pushing the issue.

"Well, at least I tried," I said smiling. "Let me know if you change your mind."

In an effort to conceal my disappointment, I chatted gaily with some of the office people, including Malik's secretary. As I left the building with him, I asked about the progress of the magazine. I was afraid that my job might be jeopardized if he detected disappointment or despera-

tion on my part. So I played along even though my problem had become mightier.

Malik's rejection of my request had sent me back to
the drawing board, and my anxiety was heightening with
every tick of the clock. I had already lost three weeks on
the twelve week countdown on my family's fate and saw no
light at the end of this tunnel.

The following week after making a delivery, I returned
home and sat at the foot of the sofa contemplating my
dilemma as I had done every night since talking to Malik.
It was at this point that a brilliant idea struck me. In a flash,
I realized that using Jun would give me direct access to a
big-time cocaine buyer in Portland, so what I could do was
steal a small part of Malik's drugs and sell them to raise the
needed money and deal with the consequences later.

Better yet, I would steal the entire shipment, deal it,
and disappear with a load of cash without having to deal
with any consequences. After all, Malik's volatility was one
thing I did not want to gamble with, and undertaking such
a risky venture would only be worthwhile if I went for the
big one.

Yes, if I had to eat a toad, I would make sure it was the
fattest and juiciest. Once I was committed to this choice of
action, I wasted no time in crafting the finer details of the
heist and committed the rest of the night to crystallizing
the plan.

Stealing the drugs would be the easiest part of it all. I
would make the pick up from the hangar as usual, but instead of taking the drugs to the houseboat, I would simply
drive to a pre-selected location and transfer the shipment
into my car and abandon the van. I would then drive south
to Portland and rendezvous with Carl whom Jun would already have contacted with the details of the deal. It would
be smooth sailing up to that point, but what to do after I

had the money was the blank spot.

I was sure there would be at least two hundred pounds of cocaine in the shipment, worth millions of dollars, meaning Malik and Torres would come after me like hounds on a rabbit.

I would have to leave the country as soon as the deal with Carl went down, which then raised the problem of getting the million or so in cash out of the country. I knew Jun, through his family, could get any amount of money safely out of the country, but entrusting all my money to Jun meant taking a leap of faith that I was incapable of. Despite our friendship, I felt that Jun was capable of appropriating the entire amount and leaving me hanging on the short end unable to return and claim the money. There was no way for me to ensure that he followed through once I was outside the country.

A viable but bold alternative to using Jun would be disguising the money as old books and sending it by courier to my sister in Kampala. I would use DHL and make sure the clerk serving me did not find out, since a package that passes that stage travels unassailed to its destination. The customs people in Uganda would not bother with the package once they saw the DHL papers. Having employed this method before in sending Anna items that ranged from clothes to CDs, I knew it to be flawless.

After sending the money, I would drive to Portland airport, book passage on a direct flight to London and be safely in Uganda in a couple of days, a millionaire. I would have to forget about Stanford and instead transfer my credits and complete my degree somewhere in Europe, probably France.

It was a lovely plan. I would learn French and vacation on the Riviera, hopefully, with Romina by my side. First, I would call her as soon as I arrived in London on my way home. I would explain everything and ask for her understanding, and then I would tell her to quit slaving and join me anywhere in the world. I would make it up to her. This was not just a promise but a heartfelt vow that I had committed to even before my father's death. It would be my statement of love.

I loved dreaming through the details of my plan. It obscured what was happening and made me confident even though I knew the realty would not be that easy. Somehow, fantasizing about instant wealth was calming and kept me from going mad. It was my self-prescribed opiate.

The following day, I caught up with Jun at the campus food court and dragged him to a corner table.

"You look tired man, what have you been up to?" he asked laying his bounteous plate on the table.

"I didn't sleep much last night."

"Reading?"

"No."

"Woman problems?"

"Nothing like that."

"Woman pleasures then, oohh."

"Will you stop bullshitting?"

"I'm just thrilled by the thought of my brave friend banging some chick all night and not showing up for an exam."

"What exam?"

"This morning's accounting exam."

"I thought that old fart cancelled it."

"He un-cancelled it yesterday. I guess you did not read the pass-down."

"No. I left early."

"You should talk to him after lunch. I'm sure he will let you take the exam from his office."

"Damn that idiot," I cursed absentmindedly, then got down to business "How much thrill would you get from making half a million bucks in a day?"

Caught off guard by the question, Jun answered with a full mouth, "A fuckin' lot of thrill. Why?"

"I'm getting the dope next week, and I need your friend Carl to be ready for it."

"It's what he does for a living. Tell me about the half mil."

"Well, instead of giving you a commission, I will let you negotiate the price with him. That way you have an interest in the whole deal, and I'm sure not to get screwed by him."

"How much dope?"

"At least two hundred pounds."

"Two hundred pounds? That's like . . ."

"Shhhh.. Keep it down mister."

"That's like four million dollars at least."

"Does Carl have that kind of money?"

"I'm sure he can find it." Jun pushed his food to the side and silently repeated the amount in disbelief.

"Listen now. All I need is half the actual value. The rest is between you and him. I will deliver the dope personally."

"How come you want very little for it?"

"That's irrelevant. I figure if this Carl dude is smart he will easily pay 2.5 since he can sell it for twice as much."

"He is smart enough to pay three million."

"Good luck for you if he pays three million. All I want is two upon delivery. He can bring your share to Seattle if he wants."

"Getting mine will be no problem."

"Good. Talk to him and tell him to be prepared with the cash next week. I will call you as soon as I have the stuff so that you tell him the exact time to expect me. You also have to arrange the meeting place."

"It will have to be the Genkai," Jun said

"The what?"

"Genkai. It's a Japanese restaurant in Portland. Probably the safest place to do the transaction. I will give you the address and directions."

"Does Carl know this place?"

"He has been there before."

"One more thing."

"What?"

"My two mil has to be entirely hundred dollar bills in ten thousand dollar bundles."

"Standard procedure."

"Plus, he has to put it in a postal shipping box and cover the money with a bunch of used text books."

"That's strange."

"It's how I want it, Jun. It has to be neat and convincing. I will have no time for any bullshit."

"Of course. If he can find the money I believe a good box and used text books will be no trouble."

After the discussion, we went to the library for a street map of Portland, and Jun showed me how to get to the Genkai restaurant near Lloyd Center, which I marked in blue ink. We also agreed that Jun would have to inspect the merchandise before he made the final call to Carl.

From the library, I went back to McKenzie Hall and talked to my accounting professor who allowed me to take the exam I had missed that morning.

One hour later, I walked to the bus stop at the 15th and 43rd Street intersection. I was glad the week was drawing to an end and along with it the winter quarter. I wondered whether I would be around for the last exam which was scheduled for the following Thursday. If my plans went smoothly, I would be out of the country by then.

Even as the prospect of millionaire-hood loomed on the horizon, I wasn't duped by its fecund duplicity. A deal such as the one I was undertaking was much like riding a cross country freight train knowing only that it was going to the coast and hoping it ended up in the city of one's choice. Along the way, the train could go in any number of directions, and there was always the possibility of derailment. Indeed, the deal could only be complete when the train finally chugged into the station of my choice. For me, this was a nice sunny day at the farm smiling and counting the money for the third time and wondering whether Romina would prefer a few weeks on the Riviera or a first class cruise in the Caribbean. Dreams, all dreams, but they could come true.

I was tired and worn out by the week. Not only had I not slept in thirty six hours, but the tension in my veins and the stress from fear and uncertainty were driving me to the point of a nervous breakdown. My neck was stiff, and I had developed a severe headache that pounded the back of my cranium as if my brain was about to implode. I desperately needed to rest before going to Romina's place that evening. First, I would shower, eat something, and take some badly needed pain medicine.

I left campus hurriedly, hoping to get home before my headache worsened. As I walked, absorbed in my little world, through campus's western parking lot to my bus stop, a middle aged, balding man stepped out of a gray Buick and asked me for directions to some place on campus. He and his passenger were looking for a faculty building they could not locate. Upon hearing my accent, he asked where I was from and seemed surprised when I told him. He was rather knowledgeable about Uganda, and we chatted for about five minutes before parting. Unfortunately, we never got around to introducing ourselves, and I didn't find out his name. My mind was too engrossed and I was desperate for the comfort of my bed.

When I arrived at Romina's place later that evening, I found her pensively watching mute pictures on television. I engaged her in small talk, and when the discomforting silence resumed, I felt the lump in my head growing again.

I was already starting to feel guilty and did not even know what I had done wrong, but I knew her well enough to tell that her sour mood had something to do with me. I asked if she would go on a short drive with me and eat out.

"I've already eaten," she said her eyes still on the mute television.

"You don't really have to eat," I said uncomfortably. "I'm hungry and I have a headache. The night air might do me good. Please."

"All right." She went into the bedroom to get her sweater and we took her car avoiding the freeway. I parked a few blocks from the restaurant so we could have a short stroll before sitting down to eat.

We walked side by side in silence, and when we were seated, I ordered an entree while she settled for a light salad.

"How was your day?" she asked while our orders were being prepared.

"OK, I guess." I found the question oddly timed but played along. "Nowadays my regular day consists of an exam and a major headache. Nothing I can't handle." We ate wordlessly, and she waited until the waiter had brought the check and removed the empty dishes before she spoke.

"Tell me, Sim, do you consider me a friend or a convenience?"

Now I knew I was in trouble.

"What's going on Romina? Why the strange questions?"

"I tried to surprise you at work today." She looked at me with distaste. "Where the heck have you been working for the last six months?" Suddenly my headache spiked and I closed my eyes to ease the pain. She had obviously found out that I was no longer working at the Madrona office or delivering the magazines as I had been telling her.

"Don't get upset please, I can explain . . ."

"I have never been dishonest with you," she said softly. "Why do you feel the need to lie to me?"

"It's not like that. I just happen to be in the middle of a complicated situation right now."

"Are you, really?" She asked looking at me thoughtfully.

The headache exploded into my temples, forcing me to clutch my forehead and stiffen my neck. The pain remained for a few seconds before receding into massive throbbing in my temples and the back of my head.

I was beginning to experience minor blank spells, so I reached into my pocket for the small bottle of tablets and popped two, following them with a drink of water, then looked at her as if she were a stranger who had just arrived at the table.

"Let me see that." She took the small red bottle and studied the prescription, then regarded me with bewilderment "How long have you been taking these?"

"About six weeks."

"What do you . . ." She tossed up her arms and leaned back in her chair frustrated.

"Why don't you talk to me, Sim? Have I become so strange to you that you cannot tell me anything anymore?"

"I wa . . ." the pain exploded once again and this time lingered longer, leaving me quivery and flushed as it receded.

When she noticed the blank spells, she paid the bill and quickly took me back to the car seating me on the passenger side. Back at the apartment, she laid me on the bed and wrapped a damp cloth around my head. I must have passed out immediately because I slumbered soundly until late the following morning.

When I finally arose in the darkened room, I had no idea where I was or the time of day, and the happenings of the previous night were a blurry mass.

She heard me fidgeting around in the room and came over.

"What happened?"

"You had a bad headache," she said, unsure if I was fully recovered. "How do you feel now?"

"No headache," I said, shaking my head from side to side to show that it wasn't hurting, "but I'm hungry."

"I thought you might be." Apparently she had called in sick at work.

I felt there was no alternative but to come clean and tell her everything. However, the need to unburden myself was coupled with a strong fear of what she might do once she knew all the facts. Would she understand the fix I was in and support my course of action, or would she reject it as uncivilized?

Could she possibly come to terms with my world with its conflicting forces edging me towards legal transgression and insanity?

I truly had no idea how to handle the situation without losing her. I decided I would tell her everything, but not at once. First, she would have to understand my dilemma. Perhaps then she would believe that my cocaine escapades were a means of last resort. Afterwards, I would tell her of my plans to steal the drugs, sell them, and leave the country, hopefully, with her by my side. If I didn't tell her something soon, I was definitely going to lose her.

Sunday was cool and overcast with clouds settling in from the coast. Although winter was holding on for a few more days, the welcome signs of spring's onset were everywhere with blossoming cherry plums and mild weather. We went for a walk south from Romina's place to a park where we sat on a picnic bench and watched joggers and riders ushering in spring. If any tension existed between us, it was due to the discoveries that she had made the previous day. I had lived that particular lie for almost six months and it had all come undone. I was nervous and could not dare to imagine what was running through her mind as she sat pensively with her hands deeply pocketed.

"My father had a big bank debt when he died," I said breaking the silence. "Now the bank wants to take everything that my family owns. Everything. It's only I who can do something about the situation." My gaze remained fixed somewhere in the near distance as I spoke. Romina listened in silence. She had always encouraged me to talk to her about my troubles, but I could never bring myself to discuss the real tragedies of my life. Certainly, not what was eating me up. She had always wanted to be the person I talked to, to be my confidante, but my impenetrable attitude had concealed my forlorn thoughts from her by a solid wall of silence.

Over the weeks since my return, I had refused to talk about my father even when she encouraged me and had instead become more withdrawn and uncommunicative. At first, she thought it was a temporary effect of bereavement that would pass, but it gradually worsened until our interactions became paltry. Now talking freely, with fear on every spoken word, I felt us reconnect on a level we had strayed from for months.

I told her what was happening to my family and allowed her a glimpse of my private world in which I was bound by ritual and uncompromising expectations.

She sensed my fear and wrapped her hand around my shoulder with encouragements and expressions of love, but my ailment was incurable.

"If the farm goes, I'm finished," I went on. "It hasn't happened and I'm already falling apart."

Despite the solemnity of the situation and the desperate need to confess completely, I could not bring myself to tell Romina that her brother and I were involved in a drug-running operation. Instead, I told her that Malik rented the van out when it was not being used at the office and needed me to drive it. The people at the office were not aware because he didn't want them knowing that he was using company property to make money on the side. I told her I was making good money doing this and had saved almost one quarter of the amount needed to pay off my father's debt, and then begged her not to bring up the issue with her brother.

"My problem is the short time left," I said. "There's no way I can raise that amount in eight weeks."

"Don't lose heart." She was sure a solution to my problem would materialize if we gave it a few days of thought, but, to me, every passing moment spelled doom. Asking me to wait for a solution was like telling me to forge the very sword by which I was about to be slain.

Chapter 8

Tuesday started normally with my usual fidgeting to turn off the alarm clock. The rain which had started the previous afternoon was persisting, so I braced myself for the foul weather before heading to the bus stop. Over the months, I had learned to anticipate Torres's fly-ins. Now I felt with certainty that tonight would be the big night and this would probably be the last morning ride I took on the bus. I had been on this ride so many times since moving to Maple Leaf, and the possibility of this being the last gave me an almost nostalgic feeling as the bus wove through the wet streets.

Along the way, I noticed strange, little details that I had never paid attention to before, like the small pink colored house or the fruit market at the first intersection. The bridge over the ravine on 15th Avenue was now much narrower in appearance, and, for the first time, I noticed how severely crumbled its sidewalk was.

Also the school building to my right suddenly looked dilapidated with broken windows. I was now a stranger riding into a new town and seeing things for the first time, and yet I could not escape the familiar aspects that had characterized every ride. First were the perennial riders on the bus.

There was the skinny woman across the aisle who always read a novel, and the black man who stared blankly at the back of her neck. There was also the old man who muttered to himself endlessly, and the redhead with earphones whom I never saw awake for as long as I rode the bus. She was always asleep when I got on the bus and still sleeping when I reached my stop.

There were two elderly women who waited at the stop in front of the school and always sat in the same seats and said the same things to each other before dozing off.

Then, of course, there was the wheelchair man in front of the guitar shop whose poodle drew the same admiring comments from the same people every morning. A few others were students like me, and they too, wore the same bored expression that I wore every morning. If this was my last ride, these memories would be permanently implanted in my mind.

My heart pounded heavily all day at school causing me to question my courage. Could I pull off the heist when the final moment arrived? I remained focused on my mission and did not want to be swayed by thoughts of the dramatic change of direction that my life was about to take.

At lunch, I conferred with Jun at the cafeteria, and we agreed that I would call him as soon as I received Torres's signal, and he would wait at a pre-arranged place to inspect the shipment. If he was satisfied, I would then be on my way to Portland to meet Carl.

I went over the street map of Portland again for what seemed like the hundredth time and mentally pictured the exact location of the restaurant where I was to take the drugs.

"Do I have to remove my shoes at the restaurant?"

"It's not that kind of restaurant," Jun assured me.

We went over the finer details. I would drive into the

parking area besides the restaurant and walk in, selecting a seat near the window where I could see the car. I would then order iced tea and wait.

"What if other people order iced tea, how will this Carl know me?"

"Don't worry, man. You won't be very difficult to notice in a Japanese restaurant." Jun was confident that everything would be fine and he reassured me repeatedly. "Stop worrying like that," he went on. "I have already talked to Carl. As soon as you are on your way, I will call him and have him ready for you. I also told him about your weird requirements. Everything is set."

"Everything better be. This is no small thing."

"Hey, you know I wouldn't blow a chance to make half a mil, don't you?"

I knew for a fact that Jun was very serious about issues that involved money and as he was sure to make an easy half million, he would make sure the deal went as smoothly as possible.

I still feared that something might have been overlooked because the deal appeared too easy. However, unable to put my finger on anything that might go wrong, I dismissed my trepidations as reasonable under the circumstances.

Before parting, we agreed that the short meeting would be at a gas station near the freeway on the Eastside. This would not only help me distance myself quickly from my employers on the west side, but would also give me ample time to ditch the van, have the drugs inspected quickly, and be on my way south in the shortest possible time.

The Chevron station on 8th Street, just off the freeway in Bellevue, was the optimal rendezvous. It was wide, well lit, and nothing would be suspicious about two guys looking into the trunk of a car. It was also only one minute from southbound Interstate 405.

When I returned to my apartment, I tried to blank out all thoughts and emotions that were extraneous to my mission, not wanting to be burdened by guilt or apprehension. I needed a clear mind.

I emptied my backpack and replaced the books with an organizer, a backup address book, and a novel, then took my passport from the bedroom drawer and put it in the front pocket of my jeans.

As I paced around the room to release some tension, my beeper sounded. I took a deep breath, held it for a few seconds, then sprang into action. First, I popped a combination of pills to keep the unyielding lump in my head from going wild, then called Jun on his cell phone telling him the operation was underway and to be at the rendezvous ahead of time. I quickly put a flannel shirt over my T-shirt, grabbed a jacket in anticipation of the endless drizzle, and took one last look at the apartment before locking the door.

I drove south towards Madrona to pick up the van, but this time I parked three blocks away from the office in a residential street. I had pre-selected this spot because it would be the most convenient from which to transfer the merchandise from the van to my car. Where I left the van was irrelevant.

Because the office was always closed when I needed the van, Malik had provided me with a spare key which I now held firmly as I ran from the parking spot to the office, darting from block to block with a miserable effort at dodging the rain.

Torres was accustomed to seeing me at the hangar within twenty five minutes of the page, so I gunned the van down the street and along the freeway to the airfield.

I arrived at the hangar in good time and started unloading the small plane that had been wheeled inside.

That day's shipment was not as large as the previous one, meaning Torres would fly in another load within the same week. I only hoped the current one was large enough to facilitate my deal. I worked hastily and completed transferring all the boxes into the van then backed out from the hangar and slid back the giant doors.

As usual, Torres said little and mostly watched me from the cubicle as I labored with the boxes. I wondered what would happen if he could read my mind. The mere thought made me quiver, but I managed to act calm in spite of mounting fear and pain in the back of my head.

Back on the freeway, I felt myself entering a strange territory that I had hitherto only mapped in my mind and knew that this was the decisive moment beyond which there was no turning back.

I continued hurrying along the freeway and turned up the hill towards where I had parked my car. By now, Torres would have alerted Mario to expect me in fifteen minutes. Luckily for me, there was an empty spot behind my car, so I backed up the van next to the car's trunk and wasted no time in transferring boxes from the van. A couple of minutes later, I noticed the headlights of a car coming in my direction a block away and thought it was probably one of the local residents driving home. I was hoping not to raise any suspicions from passersby as I worked diligently under the rain. The car continued through the cross street onto my block and slowed down close to where I was and then stopped next to the van.

I slammed shut the trunk thinking it was some confused idiot asking for directions, but the two men who emerged from the car, dressed in dark overcoats did not ask for directions. In fact they were not strangers, but the same two men I had given directions to a faculty building a few days earlier. I was completely taken off guard and had no idea how to relate to them at this point. The thin one yelled at me to step away from the cars as they both flashed their badges and pistols in unison and said they were federal agents. The fat one, whom I had spoken with a few days earlier, said nothing but opened the back of the van and removed a small plastic bag from one of the boxes and punctured it with his little finger. After testing it, he nodded to his partner. I tried hard not to freak out but still could not understand a single word of what the thin agent was going on about as he handcuffed me and removed everything from my pockets. In a few minutes, a dark van arrived and three similarly dressed men emerged from it and accosted me with the ritualistic introduction. One of them, who appeared to be in charge, asked the first two some questions and then he and another of the new arrivals led me into the back of their van which was equipped with sophisticated looking gadgetry and monitors.

I have never felt as intensely horrified as I did when I was led into that van. My entire world had just come to a screeching dead end, leaving me a wretched, sobbing and pleading mess. In addition to the fear, I felt violated as it sank in that they had followed me for days, perhaps even months, and knew everything about me.

I, on the other hand, had no idea what kind of trouble I was in or what to expect. Somehow, I wished I had learned the fat agent's name on our first encounter, perhaps then I'd appeal to him for mercy on a personal level. After all, we had talked about Uganda. He seemed like a nice guy and would know that I was not the kind of criminal scum they picked off the streets daily. Or was I?

The agent in charge lost no time in telling me exactly what kind of fix I was in and said the only way I could save my skin was by helping the FBI bring down my employers and a few others involved locally in the drug ring. I jumped at the offer of a way out since it was obvious that my options were limited. The other agents transferred the drugs I had put in the trunk back into the van. The agent in charge then led me to the passenger side of the delivery van while he took the wheel and told the others to follow us to a nearby gas station.

I was puzzled by this whole scene and it took me awhile to realize what the detective was up to. Within a few yards of the station, he stopped the van and reached under it and loosened a stopper on the bottom of the gas tank spilling most of the gas, then he replaced the stopper and unlocked my handcuffs telling me to fill up the tank and complete the delivery.

I rolled the van the remaining yards into the gas station and quickly pumped the gas and paid cash, not forgetting to request the receipt from the cashier. For good measure, I also bought a soda and rushed back to the van. The detective in charge gave back only my driver's license and reminded me that I was being watched and then dismissed me. In his hasty search, the thin detective had missed the front pocket where my passport was and had only taken my wallet and backpack. Having the passport in my possession was reassuring.

At the houseboat, I saw anxiety in Mario's eyes, but he did not ask any questions. Together we moved the boxes into one of the inner rooms after which Mario made a quick phone call before embarking on verifying the merchandise. My heart was on the verge of explosion as I watched, terrified that Mario might notice the bag the detective had punctured. I sat in one of two chairs in the outer room gently massaging my stiff neck and watching Mario take his time checking the drugs.

When he seemed satisfied, he covered the boxes with a tarp from one of the rooms and told me to wait for Malik who wanted to speak with me. I was on the brink of a nervous breakdown and keeping calm or even pretending to be fine was only straining me further. My head was like a massive boulder pounding constantly and leaving me without energy even to move about the room. I sat and waited for my boss.

"What happened?" Malik asked pulling the second chair close and observing me penetratingly. I knew the question was in regard to the time lag between my leaving the hangar and arriving at the houseboat.

"I ran out of gas."

"How did that happen?"

"There was no gas in the van. I did not realize it until the warning light came on, by then I was on the freeway, and I did not think I could make it up to here."

"Are you saying Meshak used up all the gas and just parked the van?" Meshak was the current driver who delivered the magazines to the office.

"I guess so."

"How come it took you long to get the gas?"

"Well, there's no gas station near here or in downtown, I had to drive to the Texaco on Tenth and Union. That was the closest." The inquisition distressed me, but I wasn't about to give up now, not after all I had been through. I had to maintain the act and be careful not to give Malik's keenness a chance to detect the lies.

"How much gas did you get?" he persisted in his assault.

"I filled it."

"How much did it cost you?"

"Um, about thirty five dollars." I produced the receipt and pretended to read it, then passed it on to him.

"Do you get a receipt every time you buy gas?"

"No, but I felt I was hoping to get reimbursed."

"Reimbursed?"

"Yes."

"By whom?"

"The office, or Meshak, hopefully." I knew I had blown it, but still maintained the confident facade. I had serious doubts that I had succeeded in fooling Malik, who obviously sensed that something was amiss. My answers had been immediate and precise, a sure sign that they had been

rehearsed or at least the questions had been anticipated. Also unrealistic was the issue of reimbursement. One had to be terribly anal to wish for a thirty dollar gas reimbursement when he was getting paid four hundred just to make the delivery. Malik knew me well enough to understand that I was not that kind of person.

"I will talk to Meshak tomorrow," he said and told Mario to hand me my cash.

I went back into the wet night and returned the van to the office feeling feverish and dreading the five block walk to where my car was parked. I wanted to rest my ailing body as soon as possible, but as if to compound my anguish, I found the three detectives in the dark van waiting for me near my car.

They made me drive to the North Precinct where they grilled me for hours. They asked me numerous questions about the drug operation, some of which I had no answers to. They asked about the frequency of Torres's fly-ins and the amount of substance he usually brought in. They also wanted information on the men who usually picked up the drugs from the houseboat, but when I told them I did not know their names, the detectives thought I was withholding information and grilled me even more. At one point in the deep night, I wanted to give up and request a lawyer, but they had made it clear that while that was my right, doing so would put me on the other side, and they would have to charge and detain me. They were as convincing as they were terrifying.

By the time they were done with me, they had gotten me to agree to check in regularly by phoning the department's automated case tracking line. They gave me a personal identification number to use when I called and programmed my voice into the system. They also told me to keep them updated with any and all information that had direct relevance to the ongoing investigation.

Most important, they told me to confer with them first when I received the signal for the next delivery. This, they said would be the cardinal point of my cooperation. They would give me further instructions at that time. Then, before dismissing me, they returned my wallet and backpack and told me to check if everything was still there.

"Tell me, son," said the detective in charge, studying me
thoughtfully. "How come you are taking these pills at such a tender age?"

"Ask my doctor."

"Well, I don't see your doctor here, so I'm asking you. Are you screwed up or som'n?"

"I'm not screwed up."

"Then what?"

I kept silent for a while, considering the detective's question. Was I indeed a screw up? Had my depression manifested itself in a most bizarre form causing me to behave like a madman? Would everything be OK if I let my mission rest and tried to rebuild my life and consolidate what might be left of my family? Would that be the wise choice at this point, or was it too late for sober decisions? If my family lost the land and along with it its past and future, would it not be my end, too?

"I asked you a question, young man," the detective's deep voice startled me back to consciousness. "Why are you taking this combination of drugs?"

"I have some stress related symptoms."

"Like what?"

"Persistent migraines."

"That's all?" the detective sounded doubtful.

"Yes."

"Whatever your problems, son, you better not screw up on this one. You know the consequences if you do, don't you?"

"I do."

"I'm glad we understand each other," he said nodding his head then he dismissed me.

I pocketed my wallet, zipped my bag, and walked through the rain to my car.

It was almost three in the morning when I returned to my apartment, and the first thing I did was to check my messages. The first was from Romina asking me to call when I returned, and the remaining three were frantic calls from Jun. Because of the hectic nature of my night, I had forgotten about Jun. I called his voicemail and left a short message, then swallowed some medicine before flopping into bed.

Chapter 9

A persistent ringing interrupted my sleep, and I struck out at the alarm clock in the usual manner. When the noise did not stop, I realized it was the telephone and let the answering machine pick it up, but on hearing Jun leaving another frantic message, I grabbed the receiver.

"What happened?" He asked.

"Take it easy, everything is cool." I feared that my phone might be tapped and could not risk the FBI knowing my plans with Jun, so I told him to meet me at the gym inside the University's intramural sports complex.

Before leaving the apartment, I made the first mandatory check-in call to a computer in the local FBI office. The computer, which had been programmed to recognize a combination of my voice and PIN, only responded to calls made locally. If I failed to call within a specified time, or if the computer detected an inconsistency between the voice and PIN, a warning alarm would be triggered inside an office in the federal building downtown, and I would be in massive trouble.

Jun, who had called from the campus, arrived at the gym first. When I joined him, we went into the TV lounge and sat in the chairs farthest from the door.

"What kind of screwed up business man are you?" he asked when we were seated.

"The kind that is still going to make you rich."

"Get serious man. I wait . . ."

"The deal is still on." I interrupted him, then fabricated some story as an excuse for my failure to show up the previous night, but Jun, who was still worked up, was reluctant to proceed with the same plans a second time.

"In case you are not aware these are very sensitive issues. I had to tell Carl that it's off."

"Call him and tell him it's on again. Find a good reason. We have to do this."

"No way."

"C'mon, Jun," I pleaded. "Just one more shot."

"If you can't pull off the deal smoothly, don't force it man. It might get dangerous."

"This time I'm covering all bases, trust me." In a state of abject desperation, I had conjured one more trick to help cure my problem. This would be my last chance to pull this thing off, but first I had to bring Jun back into the picture, meaning I had to juice up the deal for him.

"How does another half mil sound to you?"

"What?"

"Instead of two mil, I will take one point five." I saw Jun's eyes brighten.

"One point five for two hundred pounds of coke?"

"Like I said, what he pays is between the two of you. All I need is my cut."

"This is too good to be true, man."

"Not if you play your part and I, mine."

"What happens if you fuck up again?"

"I told you all the bases are covered this time."

"OK, when is the next magic call?"

"Tomorrow or the day after. Same arrangement as before."

"Fine, I'll call Carl tonight."

After talking to Jun, I drove to the University Bookstore and bought a birthday card, which I addressed to Anna in Kampala. I also included a small note in the card telling her to check at the DHL office for a package at the end of the week, then I walked the short distance to the post office and mailed the card.

Our birthday was in four days, and Anna had faxed me the previous weekend saying she would spend it at the farm where she had been all week. Her doctor had recommended that she get plenty of rest because she had developed complications. Although Anna never mentioned how difficult her life had become, I easily identified with the pain she was enduring. After all, she was in the middle of a difficult pregnancy and, at the same time, had to come to terms with the impending loss of the estate. I wished I could reassure her and make the suffering disappear, but that was impossible for now. The best I could do was mortgage my life and freedom to a sinister contrivance that had little chance of saving the day.

From the post office, I made another check-in call to the FBI computer and then called Romina to make sure she was home before I drove there. I was like a lone proton orbiting the empty nucleus of a miserable life and dreaded spending the night in my apartment. I longed for Romina's companionship, knowing her presence would be comforting when darkness fell.

Now trapped in a pan opticon parallel, I constantly cautioned myself knowing that somewhere out there, men in concealed cars were watching my every move and heeding a computer that could turn me into a fugitive.

Since traffic had peaked, I avoided the freeway and used the side streets, constantly looking in the rear view mirror and wondering which of the numerous cars behind me was the dreaded one. I couldn't live like this. In fact, this was not living, but dying torturously. The detectives had made it clear that the next shipment would be the last, and they

would shut down the drug ring since they now had sufficient evidence. They would then reward me with lenience, but I wasn't fooled by their sweet offers and knew I was screwed no matter what. If I cooperated fully, I would still face the lessened sentence of one or two years' imprisonment and inevitable deportation. Worse still, the farm would be gone. If I chose not to cooperate, I would be sent to prison for a very long time and still the farm would go. My only option, which was even more dangerous should it fail, was to walk the very thin line between the first two. I would create the illusion of cooperation and then disappear in a mist, leaving the two parties to sort themselves out. Indeed, I would have to be a magician to pull this one off, but it was my last card, and I had to play it, hoping only that at the end of the day, I would not have the misfortune of facing the wrath of the law or that of my less indulgent ancestors.

I joined Romina in the living room.

"Hi, stranger."

"Stranger?" I said noting her persistence in calling me stranger "I prefer my old pet name."

"Which one? Gubber?"

"Bunny wabbit."

"I have a birthday present that will blow your mind."

"What is it?"

"Patience. You'll love this one."

"A hint at least?"

"Have some patience. You'll get it on your birthday."

"C'mon, don't be mean." I rushed into the bedroom

looking for wrapped packages.

"Don't bother," she assured me and laughed at my frantic searching "It's well hidden"

When I gave up searching, I remained in the bedroom and tried to read for the following day's exam but, unable to concentrate, I pushed the books aside and lay on the bed.

"I thought you were reading," she asked, walking in from the living room.

"I've read what I need to know."

"How many exams do you have left?"

"Tomorrow's is the last." I signaled her to join me on the bed. "Can I ask you a big favor?"

"Yes."

"It's kinda weird though," I warned.

"It won't be the first."

"I need you to help me rent a car tomorrow evening."

"What for?"

"I'm going to Portland. I don't want to use my car."

"What's in Portland?"

"I'm going with Benya to check out some friends from back home."

Because Benya and I were under twenty five, we could not legally rent cars. Romina had helped us twice previously when we went to Mount Hood in the late fall, and also when we visited the University of British Columbia in Vancouver.

"So what's weird about that?"

"That's not all. After you get the car, park it at the Bellevue Mall on the third level."

She eyed me wondering what mischief I was up to.

"Make sure all windows are rolled up and all doors locked except the rear passenger door, then leave the key and this in the glove compartment." I handed her a sealed envelope that contained my passport.

"What's in there?"

"A friend's passport."

"What mischief are you guys up to?"

"Just some birthday scheme I'm cooking up."

"How am I going to drive two cars?"

"There's a car rental next to the Mall. You don't have to go far."

"But I hate Eastside traffic. It will take me forever to get back here."

"I will make it up to you."

"Massage?"

"Deep tissue"

"You are evil."

"I know."

Later that night as we lay sleepless, I asked her if, given a chance, she could settle down in another country.

"It depends. Why?"

"Would you live in Africa, for instance?"

"Not by myself."

"How about with a stranger?"

"I'd live anywhere with my stranger."

Chapter 10

The call from Torres came at five o'clock the following evening. I called the detectives immediately after, and they asked me to drive to the North Precinct where they searched me again and retained my wallet, leaving only my driver's license. They also took my pills, despite my objections, saying everything would be returned to me afterwards. They gave me two pen-like cameras and showed me how to activate them and where to place them inside the hangar and the houseboat.

Their plan was to follow me closely and monitor the hangar from inside their van. They would wait for Malik and Torres to show up together, and would apprehend them and then drive to a spot near the houseboat and wait for Gemma's men to show up, too.

Before entering the hangar, I switched on the first camera, which was inside my breast pocket, and adjusted the jacket so as not to obstruct it. Then I slid open the giant doors and drove the van inside and closed them again before I started loading the van. When I was sure Torres wasn't watching, I placed the camera in a crevice between the wall and one of the doors, which was partly concealed by the open doors of the van. When I finished loading the van, I opened the gates again and closed them behind me, leaving the camera with a perfect view of the hangar's interior.

I left the hangar and drove along the narrow road that

leads out of the airfield, trying to pick out the FBI van in the shadows. As I approached the gate, Malik's car passed me as it entered the grounds. I knew he had seen me, although he did not stop. I rarely found Malik at the hangar on the days when I picked up merchandise.

Most times when I saw him, he was arriving as I was leaving. I felt that my employ with him would have been terminated within the next few days anyway since it was obvious he did not fully trust me after the incident with the gas running out on the previous delivery.

The issue of Malik terminating me was moot. I had no intention of being around to be fired. Besides the FBI was onto him, too. Either way, the whole enterprise was winding down tonight, and I had my own plans.

I drove almost three hundred meters from the airfield before the next car behind me showed up in the rear view mirrors. I naturally assumed it was the feds and tried to maintain some distance in order to stand a good chance of eluding them. Shortly, I merged into the northbound lanes of the freeway and gunned the van along in the outermost lane, hoping to put as much distance as possible between me and my pursuers who would assume I was following the usual route.

Although there was no rain, the freeway was wet from the day's downpour, and I had to run the wipers at full force to clear the windscreen of the blinding mist and slush thrown backwards by the vehicles in front of me. I maintained calm and control, my eyes darting between the wet road and the driving mirrors as I boldly whizzed past the freeway exit that led west to the houseboat. I continued along the outer lane, which half a mile ahead would turn into eastbound Highway 520 and carry me across Lake Washington into Bellevue on Seattle's Eastside.

The mall was open for another half hour when I arrived, and there were many cars still parked on the first two levels. I passed them and continued upwards along the circular ramp to the third parking level, which had fewer cars. I brought the van to a screeching stop when I saw the brown Plymouth Acclaim parked exactly where Romina said it would be. I quickly parked adjacent to it and opened the rear passenger door. The key and envelop were in the glove compartment along with a short note from Romina, which I read quickly and shoved with my passport into my back pockets.

Without wasting time, I opened the trunk and went to work transferring the boxes from the van into the small car. Five minutes later, I locked the van and left in the rental making sure to throw the van's key in a flower garden down the street.

Jun's car was parked near the pay phones at the appointed gas station. When I pulled up next to him, he did not waste time in asking questions but walked with me to the back of the rental.

"Shit," he exclaimed when I opened the trunk "This is way more than two hundred pounds."

"I know," I said. "We are still on, aren't we?"

"Of course." Jun selected three boxes randomly and punctured them with his key.

"This is top grade stuff man," he said, rubbing some of the powder on his gums. "This has to be worth like five mil."

"At least five," I said confidently. "All I want is one point five."

"Done." Jun slammed shut the trunk. "Just proceed as planned."

"OK, see you around."

"You look very tense though. Is everything OK?"

148

"Everything is as planned. Don't worry," I tried to reassure him.

"Everything better be OK man. Don't forget any of the details."

"I won't."

We left the gas station simultaneously with Jun turning right and heading up 8th Street while I made a left and followed the blue and red signs leading to the 405 Interstate which would take me twelve miles south to Interstate 5. I fastened my seat belt and checked my watch. The ride from Seattle to Portland on Interstate 5 usually takes three hours by day. Since night traffic was lighter, I expected to make the trip in less than two and a half hours and, if all went well, I would be at the Genkai by midnight, ordering iced tea and lemon.

The migraine began mildly in the back of my head then spread into the temples. It was still tolerable, however, as it was not pounding, only dull and irritating. What concerned me was having to wait until I reached Portland before I could get some medicine from a drug store because the detectives had taken my pills.

After driving awhile, I checked the clock and realized it was ten minutes after my check-in time, meaning I was officially a fugitive. By now, all parties would have realized that I was AWOL, and I was sure a police bulletin on me was out already. The mere thought of a federal manhunt increased the pain in my head.

To stop it from worsening, I tried to push the fearful thoughts out of my mind by thinking only good thoughts. I remembered the note Romina had left me in the glove compartment, a short poem by Neruda. Leaving small notes and poems was her little game. I always found them in the strangest places and liked it because it meant we were on good terms. One day, I found a poem in my organizer, written on a check to me and signed by her. It said she was paying for love with her heart. She reminded me often how I possessed her heart, which she had given as an expression of her deep feelings for me.

Despite our frequent woes, I knew she really loved me. By allowing me to experience her, she had initiated me into manhood, and then patiently molded my boyish feelings to a mature, adult relationship. Now, I knew, would be a good time to take those feelings even higher. I would get my family issues out of the way and then ask her to join me anywhere in the world for a vacation of her dreams. Afterwards, we would settle down somewhere nice and see what life brought our way.

As I came out of a long curve south of Chehalis, I saw a patrol car parked in the median between the south and north bound lanes and reflexively shifted my foot from the gas pedal to the brakes while simultaneously checking the speedometer. It was hopeless. I had been doing at least ninety miles an hour, exceeding the posted limit by almost twenty points. I checked the rearview mirror nervously, and when I saw flashing red and blue lights, my heart sank.

"Shit, shit, shit." I banged the steering wheel and cursed myself for being so careless. When the lights persisted behind me, I found a convenient place to pull over on the shoulder.

The police car stopped behind me with its bright headlights beaming into my rearview mirror, which reflected directly into my face. My heart was now beating out of control and my mind leapt back and forth between thoughts of a trunk full of cocaine, the FBI on my trail, and endless years in prison. How could it all come together like this? Now I was really done for.

When the officer took his time coming to the car, I

became quite panicky and seriously considered jamming my car into gear and making a run for it. The idea was very appealing. After all, the cards were stacked against me.

If the policeman checked my driver's license, he would find out that I was wanted in Seattle. If I said I had forgotten my card at home, he might find cause to search the car. Whereas I was really tempted to fly off, I was aware that my purely functional Plymouth, which didn't even have a cassette deck, would be no match for the souped up Crown Victoria behind me. I tried to construct an excuse for speeding but failed to coordinate my thoughts and sat staring blankly, resigned to my fate. The officer arrived and knocked on the window, which I lowered.

"Hello officer," I said, unsure what to do and blinded by the flashlight.

"What's the rush young man?"

I tossed up my hands helplessly and said nothing.

"Driver's license and proof of ownership please."

"I handed over my license, then reached into the glove compartment for the rental receipt which had both mine and Romina's names. The officer studied the driver's license first then went back to the patrol car.

I sat shaking nervously and occasionally glanced at the blinding headlights in the rearview mirror wondering why the officer was taking forever to book me. It seemed pretty obvious that he had uncovered something and was probably notifying the FBI or calling for backup or something. It was definitely not good. When they took me in, I would remind them that I had cooperated. I would make sure I told my lawyer about my family, my dead father, and the burial grounds. The judge would surely understand that I was not a criminal and had hurt no one but was only trying to save my family from annihilation. Anyone would do the same.

The flashlight returned to my eyes, and I heard the voice of the officer but wasn't sure what he had said. Perhaps he had told me to step out of the car or just read me my rights. I was not sure.

". . . all current," the officer concluded and handed back the driver's license then gave me a document to sign. I scrawled my name and waited for an order to step out of the car and have the handcuffs slapped on me. Instead, the officer gave me a copy of the document and told me to drive safely and walked back to his car.

The red and blues flashing behind me died, and the officer drove off, leaving me traumatized.

It took a good five minutes before I composed myself and returned to the freeway paying as much attention to the speedometer now as I did the road.

Lloyd Center in the heart of Portland is a gigantic shopping and entertainment complex sitting on the eastern bank of the Willamette River. I arrived there after midnight and crossed 15th Avenue, which separates the complex from the Genkai restaurant on Clackamas street. The cityscape was generally dry, but the temperatures were low, forcing me to switch on the heat, which aggravated my migraine. I decided to complete my deal before looking for a drug store.

The Genkai was located, as Jun had described it, at the end of a long block of retail shops and restaurants, and had parking space in the front and at the sides. However, because of the late hour, there weren't many cars outside the restaurant. I parked my Plymouth in the farthest spot on the open side of the restaurant and walked in.

The inside of the restaurant was L shaped with a cocktail lounge in the back. A narrow corridor that led to the restrooms and emergency exit separated the bar and dining areas. The lounge, which also doubled as a dance floor, was dimly lit with soft colored neon lights and cushy lounge seats in which tipsy patrons sat watching karaoke.

The dining room, now nearly empty, was amply decorated with sumi art and ancient laquerworks, rendering a feel of sub-cultural authenticity. I sat in the dining area at a window booth where I could keep an eye on the car. I massaged my temples softly as I waited.

Shortly, a waitress came to my table and asked with a heavy Japanese accent if I was ready to order. I openly stared at her thinking she was one of the most beautiful women I had ever seen. I ordered iced tea with lemon and watched her glide away, leaving me overcome with a sense that everything was the surreal brought to life.

Could it be that what had been mere images in my mind over the past few days were now real events occupying time and space? How many times in the last three days had I driven into Portland and walked into the Genkai? And how many different ways had I pictured what it would look like on the inside or what face I would wear when I ordered iced tea and lemon? Could I pull off a James Dean when I made the order or would a god fatherly demeanor suffice? How about the Shaka Zulu scowl? Many scenarios had played out in my mind, and the current one might as well have been one of them, but it wasn't. What had been farfetched thoughts before were now actual events. I felt consoled by the mission's success so far but that alone could not diminish the anxiety and stress which for days had deprived me of appetite and caused me constant pain and fear.

The waitress returned with my order, then sat opposite me in the booth.

"You must be Sim," she said with an angelic smile.

"I am."

"Give me the key to your car." Her teeth were the most beautiful I had ever seen.

"I don't suppose you are Carl."

"No." Again her well moistened lips curved into a blinding smile as I handed her the key. I felt oppressed by her beauty and couldn't possibly deny her any request. If she had asked for my head, I would have offered it gladly which, after all, was killing me. I wondered if she was really a waitress or something much more. Looks like hers wer lethal, especially in a business transaction involving men, for no man, however astute, could stand his ground against such lethality. You simply went along.

She took the key and glided out of the restaurant to the car where she opened the trunk and stared inside for a moment, then closed it without touching anything and returned to the seat opposite me.

"Do you want to count it first?" She asked so casually that she could have been talking about her tip.

"No need." I was dying to know what the connection between her and Jun was, but couldn't voice the question. She couldn't possibly be his relative, which would be disappointing. She belonged in a lover's arms day and night, and if that son of a gun Jun, had slept with her yet, he would surely have already lived a fulfilled life.

My gaze followed her into the back of the restaurant. She emerged a few minutes later pushing a small handcart with a medium size shipping box on it. Behind her was another Japanese girl carrying two larger empty boxes. They went straight to the car and loaded the trunk's contents into the two empty boxes and put them on the dolly, then put the white box inside the trunk and shut it. The second girl wheeled the dolly into the back of the restaurant and the angelic one returned to the seat opposite me and slid me the key.

"The tea is on the house," she said sweetly as if she knew I was penniless.

"What's your name?" I asked, still smitten.

"Reiko." The smile again.

"Thanks, Reiko." I stood up and left the restaurant astounded by the simplicity of the deal. Two blocks away, I turned into a motel lot and examined my cargo. The box had old school books on top of neatly stacked dollar bundles. Having never seen that much money before, I was caught off guard, almost shocked. While I had tried to anticipate this, it was quite strange staring at a box full of a hundred dollar bills. I could not believe my eyes. I counted ten rows by fifteen and ten deep. Jun had indeed delivered.

What struck me as odd was that I hadn't met Carl. Could Carl have been an illusory figure created by Jun to shield his own enterprise in cocaine? Or had Jun changed plans after realizing the potential profit in selling the dope himself?

Whoever or whatever Carl was became irrelevant to me. What I cared for at this moment was that I had a box full of dollars. I closed the trunk and drove away to find an open drug store.

Chapter 11

No drug store was open in the whole of Portland at that late hour. At two o'clock I went to a 7 Eleven and bought Tylenol, which I knew wouldn't do much but hoped it could ease some of my pain. Also, I desperately wanted to talk to Romina, even if it meant interrupting her sleep, so I bought a calling card at the same store and called her from an outside phone.

She answered on the second ring.

"Sorry for waking you, dear," I said, noticing her sleepy voice.

"Where are you?"

"Not far from you." I couldn't tell her where I was for fear that the people looking for me might have tapped her phone as well. I would wait until morning and call her at work where no one interested in my whereabouts would be listening.

"Why are you calling this late? Are you OK?"

"I'm fine. I miss you."

"At two in the morning?"

"I miss you all the time, but never like now."

"Will I see you tonight?"

"I will call you at work to discuss the weekend. I have a surprise that will blow your mind."

"Are you sure?" she asked with a touch of excitement

"Give me a hint."

"You'll have to wait until morning. Right now I just want you to know that I love you no matter how strangely I act."

"I love you, too."

"Also, you should know that you are a friend and have never been a convenience."

"I'm sorry I asked you that."

"You had every right. Sometimes I send the wrong signals. I hope you understand that."

"Of course I do."

"Sleep tight. I will call you in the morning."

I dismissed the thought of finding a place to sleep immediately as I was not eager to leave my cargo unattended for a single minute. I knew of a nearby youth hostel which was open all night, but if I went there, I would have to leave the money in the car or carry it into the hostel, which was out of the question. So I parked in the lot of an apartment complex and went to sleep in the car.

One problem I had overlooked was the extremely low temperatures which assaulted me when I turned off the engine and tried to sleep. Not even my leather coat could keep me warm, so I switched on the engine again and cranked up the heat. But to avoid attracting attention from the apartments' residents who might call the cops, I could not keep the noisy engine running for long. I would run it for about three minutes to warm the cabin sufficiently and then switch it off until the freezing cold hit me again.

In so doing, I spent all night awake, and when day light returned, I looked disheveled, with bloodshot eyes and an agonizing migraine.

At first light, I drove to a nearby drug store and waited a couple of hours for it to open, then used some of the money from the box to buy extra strength pain pills and swallowed several in defiance of the prescribed dosage. Later I located a DHL office through the yellow pages and arrived there fifteen minutes before the office opened, but my anxiety returned with the fear that the DHL staff might find out what I was shipping and seriously impede my mission. Sending any amount of cash was unacceptable by the company, and if I sealed the box before taking it in, they would open it to confirm what was inside. The best I could do was try to be as deceptive as possible under the circumstances, and also hope for some luck. If I failed at this office, I would try another DHL location.

I opened the trunk and took seven bundles of cash from the box and stuffed them in my jacket and trouser pockets and then examined the contents of the box one last time before carrying it confidently into the DHL office. I picked two forms from a pile on the counter and filled one out, indicating that I was sending personal books to Uganda and addressed it to my sister. On the back of the second form, I scribbled a note to her and buried it inside the box then pressed the small silver bell on the counter. A female clerk came from the back office and took the form I had filled out. While she studied it, I nervously pushed the box towards her. She opened it and looked through it briefly. My heart missed a few beats.

"All done with school, I see."

"Oh yes. Time to send the books home."

"You can get good money by selling them back to the school. Most people do that."

"Yes, but my kid brothers and sisters need them, too."

She weighed the box and engaged me in meaningless conversation while she filled out the official section of the form. Afterwards, she fed the details into the computer, and then asked if I was from Uu-gaa-nda, reading the name off the monitor.

"Yes, I am."

"Is that like, near Nigeria?"

"Not really."

"Oohkay," she said nodding her head. "I used to know an artist guy called Peter Koy or Koye, something like that. Do you know him?"

"I don't think so. Is he from Uganda?"

"I don't know, but he is also from Africa. He's sort of famous around here." She sealed the box firmly with thick tape and pushed it into the back office, then gave me the bill which I paid in cash.

I walked back to the car with a lightened spirit, not believing how beautifully my mission was progressing. Even though the relief I felt was not total, there was no doubt in my mind that the money issue was now complete, and Anna would receive the package in a few days. I folded the airway bill and put it inside my jacket and drove toward Portland International Airport.

I went directly to the British Airlines desk, but it was empty since their flights to London left only in the evenings, so I shuffled on to the United Airlines desk and bought a ticket to Heathrow on a direct flight departing in two hours.

After paying for the ticket, I rode the shuttle to the concourse and went into the bathroom where I counted the money left in my jacket and pants which came to just over sixty thousand dollars. I had decided earlier that keeping some cash on me would be wise since the possibility of my cargo not reaching Anna still existed. I reorganized the money and stuffed some of it inside my jeans so it would not be detected when I walked through the security gate. Afterwards, I went to the duty free shop and bought a carryon bag and five hundred dollars' worth of unneeded items so that I would not raise suspicions by traveling empty handed on an international flight.

By the time I finished my mini buying spree, I was starting to feel dizzy. I thought part of the reason was that I had not eaten in hours. Although I was not hungry, I went to the McDonald's in the terminal's food court and struggled with a muffin breakfast, which I forced down with coffee and another pill. Afterwards, I called Romina's number at the bank where I hoped the lines were secure and I could talk to her freely.

The woman who answered the phone, a familiar voice, said Romina hadn't arrived at work yet, probably due to the morning downpour in Seattle. I looked at my watch, wondering what could have delayed her, then called her apartment just in case, but I was greeted by a busy tone. I waited around the phone and tried again five minutes later and still got the busy tone. I hung up and decided to wait half an hour before calling the bank again.

From the food court, I walked wearily towards my gate wracked by chills, drowsiness from sleep deprivation, and a relentless headache.

At the security gate, I pushed my bag through the x-ray machine and stepped through without incident, then went into the toilets a last time and transferred all the money on me into the carryon bag and proceeded to the lounge. I sat down and closed my eyes, hoping for the hour left before boarding to pass quickly.

The boarding announcement woke me. I thought I had only napped for a minute. My eyes were now red and teary. I rushed to the telephones to call Romina before boarding, but the man who answered the call said she hadn't showed up still and hadn't called.

My heart started racing again worrying about her. I called the apartment once more but still got the busy tone. As I took my place in the boarding line, I fought off thoughts of her being in danger. I would call again as soon as I had the chance on the plane or when I reached Heathrow.

The air inside the plane was warm, so I removed my jacket and threw it into the overhead compartment together with my bag. My seat was in the middle column of the 777's economy class. I had considered buying a first class ticket but changed my mind after thinking about the attention a disheveled black youth might attract traveling in such style with next to no luggage. I settled for economy and hoped the nine hour trip would not aggravate my condition. My eyes were heavy, and I felt dizzy if I kept them open for long in the warm cabin air. After sitting, I secured my seat belt then closed my eyes hoping to sleep. The soothing drone inside the cabin and the sound of passengers going by to their seats helped ease the dizziness. Slowly, I began drifting into sleep and dreamily heard the captain announce that he was waiting to be cleared by traffic control before pulling away from the gate.

I felt tiny twitches in my back and neck as the tension in my veins eased, and, just when my heart was starting to slow down enough to allow my system to plunge into a much needed slumber, I heard noises in the aisle and lazily opened my eyes only to see the two faces that had haunted my restless nights and my waking hours. The thin one walked down the left side while the fat one used the right aisle beside my seatmate.

"Going somewhere, Simon?" the fat one asked sarcastically and motioned for me to stand up, then read me my rights before handcuffing me. The thin one reassured the aghast passengers that everything was fine and there was no cause for alarm. Then he asked if I had any luggage, but

I was too dizzy and confused to reply to any of the questions, so they led me off the plane. In my pocket was my driver's license, passport, and the phone card I had used to call Romina. Locked in the overhead compartment were my jacket and the carryon bag with over sixty thousand dollars in cash.

The two led me out of the terminal holding me firmly to keep me from falling because I was close to passing out.

They walked me to the gray Buick and tossed me into the back seat with my hands cuffed in front of me, then the fat agent excused himself to make a phone call and returned a few minutes later. In no time, we were back on the freeway heading to Seattle.

Leaning in the back seat and slipping in and out of consciousness, I closed my eyes to keep out the light and tried to fend off motion sickness. Any fear I might have had up to this moment had vanished, and I wished for the physical pain to go away, too. I had no idea where my life was headed or what part of hell I was about to enter, but I was certain it was coming. There were no more smart ideas, no more will. I was at the end of my rope with no slack left.

The rain beat gently against the glass as we drove in silence listening to talk radio. Dreamily, I pictured the wet streets in front of Seattle's Federal Building, wondering how long they would keep me there before sending me to prison. Would I survive years of jail? Would Romina cry when she saw me?

Would she visit every week or would she give up on me? Would Anna be happy with her baby at the farm?

I went blank again and when I came to we had pulled over the freeway and the fat agent was outside the car talking briskly on the phone in the light rain. I heard the skinny one muttering under his breath clearly irritated either by his counterpart's secretive behavior or the delay it was causing. After returning to the car and driving a few miles the fat agent said we had to stop for gas. We turned off the freeway and stopped at a gas station and he went inside the store.

While he was there, a red truck pulled into the station and stopped at the pump next to the Buick. My eyes wandered towards the truck, and I recognized the driver as one of the men I had seen at the houseboat on several occasions. At first, I thought I was mistaken or perhaps hallucinating, but when I noticed that his passenger was Malik, I knew something was terribly wrong. Malik stepped out of the truck and came around the front towards the Buick.

The thin agent, who appeared to have recognized him too, opened the passenger door and began un-holstering his gun when he saw Malik remove a pistol from his jacket.

Before the agent could do anything, Malik discharged two rounds, striking him in the neck and head and then fired two more rounds through the door into the back of the Buick where I was seated helpless.

The first round hit me in the chest and slammed me hard into the opposite door, and the other one went through my right hand and lodged in my lower abdomen. I started choking and wanted to cough, but the pain was unbearable and the breathing hard. I felt like something was pushing my stomach in, and I stepped onto the driver's seat with both legs and pushed trying to ease that pain. Everything started fading as all my energy went into my legs.

. . . as I choked, I heard my mother's voice. She was coddling me and feeding me sweet gravy. I was seated in a woven crib wearing a red bib, and she had a spoon in her hand. Then I saw a river and wanted to swim in it, but I was too young and in my father's arms. I

told him something but he just smiled and spoke unintelligible words. I choked again and begged for water, but the adults did not listen. I tried to free myself and crawl towards the river but could not leave his arms. Then my mother took me into soothing hands and gave me some milk. It was warm and sweet . . . must be dreaming, I thought between labored breaths. Yes, this must be the sweet dream called life, a dream of bountiful rejection and painful mortality. In the dream, I heard sirens, then saw flashing lights and fuzzy faces wet from the rain. Then I was carried through the rain and it washed away my blood and along with it my sins.

Chapter 12

The Blue Gate house where we lived until age seven was located in a southerly suburb of the city near the military hospital. It had a big, walled-in yard, a high water tank in the back corner of the compound, and a two room servant's quarters where the maid stayed. The gate was a bright aquamarine with a small clearance at the bottom through which the dog escaped nightly to eat from the garbage bins down the street. When we were older and had moved, we referred to it as the Blue Gate house because that was the most memorable physical aspect about it.

Our parent's room was separated from ours and the guestroom by the living room and a door that led directly into a corridor connecting their room and bathroom. I remember the nights being very warm in our room because the sun shone directly into our window every afternoon. Because of this, our mother insisted that we keep the curtains shut.

Unlike my sister, I do not have vivid memories of the years at the Blue Gate house. We were very young and just starting school, and our parents went to work every day. Except for pockets of obscure memories, I don't recollect much about that time of my life. I remember the kindergarten Anna and I attended. I remember the swing tires and that the chairs in the advanced kindergarten class were red and bigger, while ours in the junior class were smaller and multi colored. But of the place we lived and what happened there, I remember very little, mostly highlights like our birthday parties and the days during the war.

The Blue Gate house became a place of mixed emotions for me as I grew older. It was the house into which Anna and I were born, and at the same time, the only real place I associated with our mother.

In many ways, it ceased to exist with her disappearance so any thoughts of the house necessarily meant thoughts of her. As I grew into puberty, I started thinking about what growing up with a real mother would be like. Many of my friends in boarding school had both parents and it was mostly their mothers who came on the monthly visiting days. On those days and other more significant ones like graduations, I wished for a real mother.

I missed the feeling of having someone appreciate my achievements in that special way that only mothers can, and while our father was always present as a parent and Auntie Drusilla an effective surrogate, I felt something was amiss.

Somehow, the forward movement of life had overtaken our mother's existence and usurped her spirit so that the mother in our family only lived in old family albums and was rarely a subject in family conversation. Perhaps this was because we were very young when she disappeared, and our father thought it would be better to move on with life. In any case, he never talked to us about her, and I never asked him about her. I knew our parents had met in the early sixties when our mother was in high school and our father in a junior college that shared a fence with the all girls' high school. I remember granny joking that the college boys used to sneak through the fence on weekends to lure out the girls.

This is how our parents came to know each other. A couple of years after our mother graduated from high school, they both secured college scholarships to study in the United Kingdom. This was a time when the young, newly independent African nations were being flooded with scholarships from Western and Soviet bloc countries.

Because there were not many people entering college in those days, it was rather easy for high school leavers to secure scholarships to study abroad. My parents spent the later part of the sixties at college in the United Kingdom and returned at the start of the seventies around the time Idi Amin became president. In those days, a government program had been implemented whereby anyone with a college degree was guaranteed a government job.

Initially, they both got government jobs with father working in insurance while mother worked in the Internal Affairs Ministry. In fact, the Blue Gate house was purchased under a government program that subsidized housing for state employees. A few years later, father left his government post and started a private company in a partnership with a friend.

The house we moved to after our mother's disappearance was built to rent out and was not fully completed when she disappeared; however, our father decided it was best to leave the Blue Gate house and its sour memories and move into the new house while the finishing touches were being added.

For father, this was a very practical decision. After all, our mother's disappearance had followed rapidly on the war months which we had spent huddled in the house. In addition to escaping whatever demons haunted him in that house, father's business had been decimated by the war and a chance to rent the house out was a golden opportunity for generating some income rather than waiting for the new home to be completed.

When we moved into the new house, the plastering on the walls was barely finished, and we had to put plastic bags and cardboard in the windows since there was no glass. The fixtures and electricity were completed several months later, as was the ceiling.

Because we experienced its incipiency, Anna and I felt a special connection to the new house. In many ways, it grew up with us and became the home that we knew until we left for college.

. . . In the middle of the night, I heard our mother shouting and I sat up in my bed. The two were quarrelling again. They had been at it every night that week. I looked over to Anna's bed to see if she had heard anything, but she was breathing heavily, obviously in deep sleep. I quickly got out of bed and stealthily made my way through our corridor to the living room and peeped through the key hole of the door leading to our parent's corridor. I saw my father standing at the bathroom door telling our mother to open it.

I could hear her sobbing and shouting, accusing him of sleeping with her sister. He banged on the door and spoke short stern sentences without being loud and then went back into the bedroom and returned with a set of keys. He opened the bathroom door and flung it inward.

I heard mother scream and then they emerged from the bathroom with our father behind her, his left arm around her neck and his right grabbing her hair.

He shoved her into the bedroom and shut the door without turning off the corridor light. I moved over to the wall their room shared with the living room and pressed my ear against it and heard mom sobbing quietly. After a while, everything quieted down and I returned to my bed.

The human mind and its infinite intricacies is indeed something that science shall never fully fathom. Personally, I think it's the ultimate barrier to human understanding of the self. An inexpungible culprit rather than a frontier. In my experience, the real obstacle to my self-examination emerged when I tried to make sense of the peculiarities my mind was conjuring. Until then, I had been confident in my mental health and pretty secure in my overall self-estimation; however, after being extensively hospitalized, my mind started spawning a morass of convoluted imagery that left me questioning my sanity and my history.

The images were nightmarish and weirdly hallucinatory, almost all about my parents and the years at the Blue Gate house. These washed over me repeatedly through my months of recovery, and the moment I tried to sort through them is the moment I ceased to understand myself.

I had awakened from a deathly slumber one day to look into my sister's face. I don't think I knew who this person was at the time, but I felt she was somehow a part of me. She had a baby in her arms and she spoke to me. Other people came into the room and rearranged me back and forth. The only sense I had at the time was vision. I really had no idea what was going on initially, but, with time, I knew I was in a hospital room. Eventually, I recognized Anna as she came in at intervals with the baby. I must have spent more time in the dream world where I saw my parents than I did in this world where I saw my sister. In any case, it took me a bit of time to acclimatize and start recognizing the real waking environment.

I had been in intensive care a full eight weeks by the time Anna arrived in Seattle. My condition had been improving steadily, and the doctors were hopeful that I would be out of intensive care within three to four weeks. Anna spoke to me every time she came to the hospital, even though I could not respond to her.

I was slipping in and out of my nightmare world and never quite knew where I was except when I saw her. I knew then that I was where she was. That was comforting. I thought she looked peaceful even though I had seen tears in her eyes on some occasions. But I was there with her and that was important to me. A doctor and nurse attended me daily and started me on a therapy routine. I was wheeled out of the room every other day and taken to see a therapist who tried to make me speak. While I felt I could, I never had the will to do so. Not even to Anna. Then the therapist made me do gestures and draw pictures.

I had a dream within a dream. . . . we returned from spending the weekend with granny on a Sunday afternoon and found our mother with bruises on her left side. She had slipped and fallen in the kitchen the day before while she was trying to get something from the top cabinet. Our father told us this when he picked us up from granny's and said we should stop by a flower shop to get her some flowers. Anna picked the bouquet and I got a card, which we both signed.

Father paid quickly and we hurried home to see her. She was in the bedroom when we arrived and was moved by the flowers and the card. Her face was still swollen under the eye and she had a bandage around her left ankle. Then we went to sleep, and at night, I felt someone nudging me to wake up and it was my mother. I was in my room in Seattle, near the university. She walked into the kitchen and I followed her, but it was the old kitchen from my childhood. My father was in the kitchen, too. They were talking animatedly, but I could not hear what was being said. I saw my father push her against the wall, then she poured coffee in his face. He punched her in the face, and she went careening into the pantry and twisted her ankle.

I tried to tell Anna that our mother was telling me things in my sleep, but she did not understand me very well. She said I had slipped into a coma again. When the doctor came, she told him I might be having nightmares, but he said it was impossible as brain activity was minimal in a coma. The issue of my dreams never came up again.

The bullet that hit me in the chest had shattered my sternum and destroyed one third of my right lung. In a seven hour operation, doctors had removed the bullet and the damaged part of the lung and started extensive reconstructive surgery on the sternum, which would require at least six weeks for the bones to begin fusing. The second bullet had narrowly missed the liver and lodged in the spine causing paralysis from the chest downward. Any attempt to remove it could only compound the damage on my nervous system, which was already compromised.

Although I had recovered full consciousness by the seventh week, I could not move any part of my body or speak coherently, and it would not be until three months later, after numerous sessions of physical therapy, that I managed to move my hands and head freely. Also, because of the paralysis, I had to wear a specially designed brace around my limp torso to support me while seated.

My world was a hospital bed and a wheel chair for several weeks after I gained consciousness. After a couple of weeks of speech therapy, I was transferred to a lavishly wooded sanatorium away from the city. By this time, I was able to communicate a little and had been apprised of my condition.

Most of the talking I did was in exercises with my therapist. I never said much to Anna and was terrified by the feeling that we had lost our ability for the internal communion we always had. At first, she and the baby were allowed one weekly visit, but when I was transferred from intensive care, they came daily for short visits. Even though I never said much to her, Anna told me stories about home and things she thought I might be curious about. Sometimes she said funny things and I smiled, but many times tears rolled down my face and I closed my eyes. When I got deeply depressed, I showed no signs of noticing her presence. She was strong around me even though my sorry state was heart wrenching. The doctor had told us my paralysis was permanent and that I was in a state of psychological trauma which could take anywhere from a few weeks to several years before it healed.

I had always been the strong one, guiding Anna when she was challenged. I had taught her how to swim in the river. In third grade, I had protected her from senior bullies and gotten badly hurt myself. I had always been there, shielding her from pain. Now my own was suppressed in unspeakable thoughts.

For the first time, my mind was impenetrable, even to myself, and I knew she could not connect with me as she had since childhood. Did she know that I recognized her as my sister, my very own flesh and blood, or was she doubtful when I spoke unintelligible words? Did she think my despair would tear me away? I was a child again now. Speaking unintelligibly and physically disabled. I so badly wanted to be with my mother, to return to her womb for warmth and protection.

The sanatorium was located an hour north of the city in east Snohomish County where I continued physical therapy and began psychiatric therapy for mental stress and manic depression. The doctors thought this might cure my speechlessness and other minor symptoms like night sweats.

Three times a week, Anna and the baby made the one hour trip from Benya's apartment in Everett, where they were staying temporarily, to the sanatorium. They would stay two hours with me on every visitation.

My only other visitors were Benya, who came a few times, and an FBI man called Mark Heinricksen who came once every couple of weeks to ask me questions. Apparently the FBI operation had been thoroughly botched with everyone ending up dead or disappearing. Malik was dead and so was gold-toothed Mario who was found hanging in his cell. The fat agent, called Ramsey, was found dead in his house, poisoned. Obviously, someone was cleaning up behind the scenes, and the FBI hoped I'd provide them with some information that may get them somewhere. Heinricksen was especially curious about the two men I had told the FBI about, the so called Gemma's men and, particularly, their boss Antonio Gemma whose name he brought up repeatedly, but I had no more information in that direction. He returned several times to see me in the hope that my recovery would help clear my memory, but I had nothing for him.

As the summer progressed, so did my mental condition. With time, I was able to communicate better with Anna and my therapist, mostly in short phrases. Often Anna wheeled me into the sprawling fields for a stroll, something that was encouraged by the nurses and that many patients did with their families or caretakers.

I liked holding my nephew on my lap while sitting at the patio or under a tree in the expansive compound of the sanatorium. I stared endlessly into his big innocent eyes and kissed him repeatedly. He brought life to my eyes and often made me laugh when he bobbed his head on my face in search of his mother's breast. It was unbelievable that life could stem from such purity and innocence then turn so ugly and painful.

The days at the sanatorium were almost always the same. The nurse usually fetched me at nine o'clock, gave me medication, and wheeled me to the lunchroom where I had breakfast with the other patients, or residents, as they were commonly called. My table was shared with two other residents I had grown attached to over the months.

Mr. Whitfield was a former science teacher who talked to his food and other inanimate things. His affliction, it seemed, was the spontaneous need to channel his voice. When he got such attacks, he would go on about this and that for hours on end and only sedation could stop him. If you interrupted him, as many residents did, he tended to get aggravated and so his solution was to talk to walls and furniture, which guaranteed full attention. Many times he talked as if to a class of kids, telling them about the wonders of science. This never came across as strange to me since I knew about his teaching background; however, when his monologues ventured into subjects like astrophysics and special relativity, I, too, would be as magnetized as the furniture being addressed.

The other person at the breakfast table was Boaz who was more popularly known by his nickname "Tiny" or "Tiny Boaz." Tiny had been at the sanatorium only six weeks and was likely to leave before many of the other people there. He was a construction worker in the small industrial town of Mount Vernon, and, despite his nickname, he stood six foot ten inches and weighed over three hundred and fifty pounds. Tiny's problem was unknown to me, but on his bad days, he ran amok and fought unseeable assailants, often harming himself in the process. When he was first brought in, the doctors had been compelled to put him in a strait jacket for two days. His condition, however, seemed controllable with a daily dosage of drugs.

Like Tiny, everyone at the sanatorium had bad days. My bad ones were mostly spent at the patio outside the lunchroom where I normally wheeled myself and sat for hours staring at the empty fields. I was still overwhelmed by emotional pain and cried often. The only part of the day I looked forward to was the brief visitations from Anna and the baby. In the evenings, the nurses took me into the physical therapy room where I worked with the sanatorium's specialist for thirty minutes. My psychiatrist's days were Mondays and Thursdays when I had no visitors.

Benya came to visit a few times with Anna and liked to bring me my old mail that he thought was relevant. The last time I saw him, he brought a newspaper in which the story about the drug bust had been run. I looked it over briefly and put it aside together with a manila envelope from Stanford University.

I did most of my reading at night, which, along with the medication, helped me transition gently into sleep. That night I looked at the bulging manila envelope from Stanford and tossed it in the recycle bin unopened. I knew it was an acceptance package but did not care for Stanford anymore. Besides, even if I had cared, the time had come and passed and so had the moment for such trivialities as the Ivy League. I was in a different universe now, humbled by life and bereft of ambition.

The newspaper was several months old and contained an article about the deadly shootings and the ensuing investigation in which the FBI was accused of a botched job. Special Agent Mark Heinricksen was mentioned by name as having taken over the investigation. Other familiar names were also mentioned. Malik had been shot at the gas station by the truck driver, and the two agents who arrested me were also dead. This I already knew from Mark

Heinricksen. He had been forthright with me, but what he had not mentioned was that the investigation had led them to Romina's house. According to the article, she was found in her apartment tied to a chair with phone wire with a bullet hole in her head. She had been dead at least three days.

. . . sometimes our mother left home and returned a day or two later wearing the same clothes. We knew this related to her work at the Ministry. The war was beginning to intensify and the artillery got closer and angrier. Sometimes she and father stayed up all night talking about the stuff she brought back. She always had documents and miniature slides that she brought back with her. When the war heated up, she stopped going out.

Anna and I slept in our parent's room during the war. Our mother wanted us beside her all the time. One night while she was gone, I woke up with a burning thirst and wanted to get a drink. Only Anna and I were in the room, so I went to the guest room where our mother's sister slept. I wanted her to get me some water from the kitchen as I could not reach the water jar atop the cupboard. Her door was slightly open and the candle burning. I heard sounds and thought she was listening to the radio, but when I pushed the door slightly, I saw her and my father naked in each other's arms. They were on the bed, facing away from the door.

After the war had ground to a halt, we started school. Our mother took us in the mornings and picked us up in the afternoon. She did not have work yet and stayed home most of the time. She cleaned the house and cooked since we had no maid. Her sister had left immediately after the war ended. She and mom had gotten into a fight and my mother asked her to leave. I had no idea where she went and she was never mentioned again.

A few weeks after her departure, I saw her in the driveway at night. From our window, we could see the gate and part of the driveway. Our father came home early those days and occasionally made us dinner and tucked us in if mother was away or not well.

That day our mother had left in the morning and was not yet back when we went to bed. In the middle of the night, I heard a car at the gate and snuck to the window to take a peek at the driveway. The car's lights were not on, and the only sound I could make out was the gentle crushing of the gravel as the car slowly came around the driveway.

Our mother's sister stepped out and walked quickly towards the garage door where I heard more sounds. A door opened and I heard her talking rapidly with our father. She returned to the car and opened the trunk, and then she and my father went into the garage and came back carrying something like a really heavy sack. Our father had a pair of red women's shoes in his hand. They put the bundle and the red shoes into the open trunk and shut it. Then she drove away without turning on the headlights.

Chapter 13

Anna told me about the complications of her pregnancy on a Friday morning as we sat at the patio. Although she had experienced several stress related problems, her health had appeared remarkably stable. However, she went into premature labor four weeks before her due date and was immediately checked into the hospital. Her condition had derived from stress endured over the previous months and from complications of placenta previa, an infirmity that almost always guaranteed premature birth. She had worried about me after receiving the huge amount of money I shipped back and had gone into labor shortly afterwards. Aisha, her friend, had been in touch with Benya at Anna's insistence and knew of my problems but had not told Anna anything for fear of compounding her condition. In fact, she had felt compelled to lie to Anna, saying she did not want her to suffer given the delicate condition she was already in.

Eighteen hours after Anna's admission into the hospital, she had given birth to a slightly underweight baby boy who was whisked away by the nurses for incubation and observation. Among those present at the birth were Aunt Drusilla who had not left Anna's side in three days, Aisha, and one of our younger cousins. Anna remained in the hospital for three days before being discharged and, twelve days later, her baby was brought home with a clean bill of health.

The environment at the farm was festive when the newborn arrived. The baby who had been born exactly four months from the day of my father's burial was believed to be his reincarnation and was called by the same names. Several relatives and friends came to bless him and sanctify the reincarnation of the soul whose passing they had mourned four months earlier. They addressed him in the same manner as they had my father, calling him by the same names and nicknames.

I was curious as to how Anna had learned of my situation, knowing it was a dark day in her life. Apparently, Aisha had sort of eased her into the news rather than telling her the details she had gotten from Benya. Anna spoke of Aisha with tears in her eyes. She was deeply moved by her friend's compassion and devotion. Aisha had endured guilt for keeping my afflictions a secret but was convinced it was the best thing to do until Anna was strong enough to handle the news, which would be after the baby was born.

Aisha had come to the farm the day after the baby was brought from the hospital and found Anna seated in the shade of the giant baobab near the milking stalls. The two had tea in the shade and talked about the baby and Anna's health before Aisha mustered the courage to unburden herself.

"When she told me you had been shot, I felt my head spinning and sat on the grass," Anna said. That evening they called Benya from Aisha's house, and two weeks later, she and the baby were on a flight out of Kampala.

That day was the first time Anna and I discussed the shooting, and she was very pensive.

"What were you thinking, Sim?" she asked me emotionally. I could see she was going to cry, but I had nothing to say to her. For the first time, she lectured me about my decision.

"Please don't think that I'm harassing you. I just need to get this off my chest." She questioned how I could throw my whole life away because of the family estate and how I could be so stubbornly backward in my thinking to put that much stock in ancestral lore? This is where Anna and I differed. She was not the one burdened by the onus of heirdom—I was. Heirdom was a thread of ancestry and it ran in my veins. Every single day of my life, I had been reminded, cajoled, lectured, and conditioned for my moment.

Not Anna. What was mere myth to her was reality to me. I was the one on the frontline, carrying the tradition forward, and soldiering on no matter the circumstances. Could Anna understand this on a visceral level? Of course not. She cared about me and my wellbeing, which is what she always did and had been raised to do. I, on the other hand, had to look after everyone. My wellbeing was not my responsibility.

I asked Anna about our mother and tried to get her to tell me things she remembered about the years at the blue gate house. She knew I had next to no memories of our mother while we were growing up, and that I was now having dreams about her. She shared her memories with me, never mentioning a bad one. I also asked her about our mother's sister.

"Oh you mean horse face," she said.

"What?" I was perturbed.

"Horse face," she repeated. "Don't you remember how we hated her and called her horse face because she reminded us of the singing horse in the animal farm cartoon?"

Of course I did not remember that, but I remembered

the dream I had after being told of my father's death. The face of the woman on the back of his head. The squealing horse.

"I remember the day mom disappeared, too," Anna went on. "She left early in the morning for a job interview. I remember very well because I had gone shopping with her the day before, and we bought a red suit and red shoes for her to wear to the interview."

My arms started trembling as the significance of her words filtered into my head. Had I dreamt her memories? Or were my own simply suppressed? I could not bring myself to tell her what weird hallucinations haunted me nightly. How could I? This was my private hell, a part of that burden which only I should carry. How could I invite her into the hellish world of my nightmares—to alter her life by disclosing what I now knew?

I hated my life and despised my father, wishing I had never been sired by him. How could mountains of love and adoration built up for the man I called father come crushing down following a few hallucinatory dreams? Could it be the multitude of medicines I was taking that were skewing my reality, blending nightmarish hallucinations with reality? Somehow, I knew that was not the case, because, in spite of the weirdness of the dreams, I had faith in them. If anything, the drugs pumped into me daily were resurrecting deeply suppressed memories going back nearly twenty years.

The nights became awful. I could not sleep and was suffocated by guilt every waking moment. I wanted to kill myself but could not poison myself, hang myself, or do anything physical in my limp state. I loathed myself. I had become some pathetic amalgamation of useless protoplasm, defecating and urinating in bags and being attended by a rotation of hag-like medics who fed me antiseptic food. I did not need this life, never asked for it, and wanted it gone. I begged for it to end and tried to negate it by will but failed at that too.

The responsibility for my extended family had been prepackaged and passed down to me, and I, too, would have to pass it to the next person. That person was my nephew. He was next in line. After all, I had no children and would never have any. He had only a mother, having been abandoned by his father before he was born. I would have to step in and raise him as my own. Indeed, he was the only remaining hope for the family, and if there was any striving for life on my part, it was to ensure that I cleaned up the demons of my family and handed my nephew a clean slate.

One morning at the beginning of November, I returned to the patio outside the lunchroom as I had many mornings before, only this would be my last. The doctors had deemed me fit for release and said I would thrive amongst family and friends. However, due to my involvement with the drug ring, a directive had been issued by the courts that I leave the country within forty eight hours of my hospital release.

So, I sat at the patio and waited patiently. This day had been five months coming. Now it was here—the very last day. Soon the sanatorium would be a memory. Its vast fields, rigid nurses, and strange residents would all be gone, and I would not miss them, not for a single moment. I sat watching the leaves blow away in the wind. The summer was now gone and the rains had returned. I looked forward to the days at the farm, spending time with Anna and my nephew. They were, after all, the only reasons I had to live.

In the early afternoon, I saw two cars come through the sanatorium's gates. The black sedan, which I recognized, was followed by a yellow shuttle van. At the first junction, they turned left and continued along the narrow leaf-littered road and disappeared behind the administration building. A few minutes later, one of the nurses collected me and wheeled me to the superintendent's office where my paperwork was processed. Mr. Heinricksen introduced the two men he was with as INS officials. They were required to escort me to the airport.

The driver helped me into the back of the van and secured my wheelchair for the two-hour drive. Anna and the baby sat directly behind him with their bags which Anna had parked before leaving Benya's apartment. In no time, the van was on the freeway heading south to the airport.

At the terminal, the INS men gave my papers to the airline officials. The airline would in turn hand me to officials of the connecting flight from London who were responsible for seeing that I was properly handed over to the officials in Uganda. We were given the bulkhead seats with ample space for my wheelchair and enough room for a small baby cot, which was provided by one of the attendants.

As the autumn night rapidly advanced, the plane pulled from the gate and slowly taxied towards the runway. I ruminated about my short role on the American stage and remembered how, only two years earlier, I had arrived on this very tarmac full of ambition and dreams. Now, here I was again, leaving, an invalid with a broken spirit and a dead will. According to my deportation papers, I was not to apply for any re-entry visa for at least seven years.

Deep inside, I knew I would never return to the United States. Here, a part of me had died, a very large part. To come back would be to kill the rest. At the far end of the runway, the plane stopped briefly, then started moving again and picked up speed. In a few seconds, I saw the ground falling away and tears filled my eyes. When Anna saw that I was overcome with emotion, she held my hand and squeezed it lightly. She, too, was weeping.

For me, America was now gone forever, torn brutally from me by forces beyond my control. It had given me vision and love, and then torn them away painfully. My best days had been lived on its very soil. Now there it was, falling away forever. Its sweet memories obscured by dreadful dreams and images.

I opened the newspaper that Benya had brought me and read the story again. ". . . tortured and shot in the head . . ."

Tears rolled down my face and fell on my limp legs. My Romina was gone, she of the tofu sandwiches and the Sunday markets, loving and harmless as the morning dew, brutally murdered for my selfishness. It made no difference that someone else had done the actual killing.

She had professed her love for me, but I betrayed and killed her.

Here I was, only twenty three years old. I would never have children of my own or dance again with a lover. No measure of money or time could resurrect the love that had died with Romina. It was a ghost now, a beautiful ghost with dark locks and sensual eyes. A recurring dream that brightened dismal nights.

Epilogue

The man hired to fix the hedge around the graves had done a shoddy job, and the cows continued to knock it down every time they passed from the milking stalls. As a result, we had to reinforce it with mud bricks taken from the neighbor's brick ovens, which was a temporary fix as the rains tended to erode them. I had been spending quite a bit of time around the graves and had decided that a brick wall should be built around them.

Anna thought it was an unnecessary expense considering the graveyard was bound to expand. She was also concerned by the amount of time I spent at the graves, thinking I was slipping into one of my perennial depressions.

One fine afternoon, she returned from school and joined me by the graves where I sat pensively in my wheelchair writing on and off. She sat on the grass next to me and started feeding the baby. He had recently started walking and had instantly developed a voracious appetite from spending much energy overturning everything in his way like a tiny Godzilla. We sat in silence listening only to the baby sounds as he fed, then she sang him a lullaby and he slept.

"I think we should move mom's monument away from dad," I said at length. "We should put her near granny."

Anna looked at me with more questions than she could ask.

"Are you sure?"

"Yes. I think she would like that."

Other books by this author:

The Bonds of War (Aalvent Books, USA)
- Wambalye Weikama

Other books from KHAMEL Publishing:

Cry of the Widow: Songs and Thorns Poem Collection Book I - Marie Pinto Nakato

Blood Prints: Songs and Thorns Poem Collection Book II - Marie Pinto Nakato

Garden Weights: An Original Stage Play - Andrew Busingye

A Greek God in Harlem - Melissa Kyeyune

Miguel and Grace - Melissa Kyeyune

Faith that Conquers - Nicholas Kisakye

www.khamelpublishing.com
** Amplifying African Texts **